The *Power of*
WOMEN

UNITED

THE ULTIMATE PUBLISHING HOUSE (TUPH)
49540 – 80 GLEN SHIELDS AVENUE,
TORONTO, ONTARIO, CANADA, L4K 2B0

Telephone: 647.883.1758 Fax: 416-228-2598
www.tuphpublishing.com
E-mail: admin@tuphpublishing.com
        felicia@feliciapizzonia.com

US OFFICE:
The Ultimate Publishing House (TUPH) P.O. Box 1204
Cypress, Texas, U.S.A. 77410

Ordering Information
Quantity Sales: COMPANIES, ORGANIZATIONS,
INSTITUTIONS, AND INDUSTRY PUBLICATIONS:
Quantity discounts are available on bulk purchases of this book for reselling, educational purposes, subscription incentives, gifts, sponsorship, or fundraising. Unique books or book excerpts can also be fashioned to suit specific needs such as private labelling with your logo on the cover and a message from or a message printed on the second page of the book. For more information please contact our Special Sales Department at The Ultimate Publishing House.
Orders for college textbook / course adoption use.
Please contact the Ultimate Publishing House
Tel: 647 883 1758

TUPH is a registered trademark of The Ultimate Publishing House
Printed in Canada.

The Power of Women United by Lia Bandola & Tina Dezsi
ISBN: 978-0-9819398-1-0
First Edition

The *Power of*
WOMEN

UNITED

Confidence Born of Strength and Wisdom

Successful Relationship Builders Share Networking Strategies

Lia Bandola &
Tina Dezsi

Tina's Dedication:

I dedicate this book to my mother and father, Ellie and John Tureck. Without their sacrifices and belief in me, I would not have accomplished half of what I have.

To my boys, Justin Miller and Zachary Dezsi, whom I love with all my heart: Thank you for always supporting me through the crazy times when I needed you the most!

To my love, Ossie Di Leva: I am blessed every day to have you in my life and looking forward to spending the rest of it happily ever after with you.

To all the women who followed their dreams before me, to the women who are currently in their self-discovery journeys and to all the young women who have yet to start their search, my hope for you is that you will find the words within these pages encouraging as you lead your own path.

Lia's Dedication:

To my parents, Teresa and Michael Paolozza, who are no longer with me on earth and who I now have as my special angels guiding me: You are in my heart forever.

To my husband, Gary, who has been by my side for over thirty years and has supported me through thick and thin: You have my never-ending love.

To my three amazing children, Aaron, Kevin, and Dana: You are truly my pride and joy, and my inspiration to be the best I can be. I love you so much.

To all my mentors and guides, living and passed: My deepest gratitude for bringing me to this joyous place in my life.

Acknowledgements:

To our publishers, Felicia Pizzonia and Sherry Wilsher: This project could not have come to light without your positive energy and sense of fun.

To Felicia Pizzonia, who came into our lives at exactly the right moment for The Power of Women United to be born: Your encouragement, support, and ongoing enthusiasm is the glue that binds this project together.

To all the contributing authors whose life journeys inspired us to use their stories as an essential tool to share with the women of the planet: Your talents and beauty are immortalized here on these pages as a beacon for those seeking their place in the world.

To our POWE sisters: You continue to encourage us to follow the dream of offering women a place to belong and to grow beyond their dreams.

To all the women of the world: Our hope for you is that you find your greatness and celebrate every moment of it!

Table of Contents

Introduction:
How This Book Came Together

The value of diversity in business is becoming more and more obvious to many of the traditionally male-dominated industries. In 2004, we realized the importance of giving women their own platform to empower themselves and improve their lives, and so emerged Power of Women Exchange. For the past five years, this organization has helped women inspire each other and achieve their dreams. This phenomenal group of women is dedicated to supporting each other in both their professional and personal lives.

As successful entrepreneurs and businesswomen, the desire to create a balance among all of the demands we face daily is no longer a luxury — it is a priority. The women you meet in The Power of Women United demonstrate their expertise, knowledge, and visions in the corporate arena as well as in their own businesses, many of which generate millions of dollars in revenue each year. Now more than ever, we are breaking away from society's preconceived notions and choosing a lifestyle that meets our needs.

Each woman in this book offers her own unique, powerful, and valuable insight on multi-tasking, leadership, and financial management, skills that ultimately helped the women to achieve a life balance. For the first time in history, more women than ever are achieving success on their own terms. They've chosen goals, followed their dreams, and become successful against all odds. As you read through these pages, you'll soon begin to realize there is a common trait among these women, a strong sense of determination and commitment, and a willingness to help others. Successful women understand the obstacles and challenges in the world today and are willing to embrace them and transform them into opportunities for advancement.

We are empowered to make a change in today's business environment and lead with integrity and innovation. We believe in sharing our success and helping others to attain it as well. Many of us are reaping the benefits and living a life of fulfillment. Each one of us possesses the confidence, skills, and talents to live the life we've always dreamed of. Those who've become successful in their careers have done so with the help of others. On average,

75 percent of referrals for new business are acquired through relationship building. These relationships are the single most effective way to meet new business contacts and mentors, and to surround yourself with likeminded individuals. Networking is the best method to do this.

We, as women, are natural-born networkers because of our innate ability to create and maintain relationships. The value of networking is in the personal connection you make with others. Organizations and books such as Power of Women Exchange and The Power of Women United are essential for our success. Each author shares her vision, mission, and values to help you find and follow your purpose in life.

Women entrepreneurs are having a tremendous impact on today's economy, and, as the founders of Power of Women Exchange, we believe the opportunity to connect with other professionals, exchange ideas, and share resources enables you to expand your horizons, learn from others, and increase your business. Networking offers an incredible amount of support for creating success in life and gives you a definite edge to move forward in your career. It does not have to be intimidating or frightening, as you will soon learn.

Successful women, who recognize that amazing things can happen much easier with team effort, freely give their assistance to help others succeed. In turn, they know they will receive support, making their own dreams a reality. So, whether you are trying to create your own business, expand your existing one, or just want to seek advice from those who've gone before you, the stories of the women in The Power of Women United will inspire you to stretch and reach your highest level of success.

For more information about what POWE has to offer, visit
www.powe.ca

Chapter 1

IDENTITY CRISIS
— ONE GAL'S STORY
BY LIA BANDOLA

Chapter 1

IDENTITY CRISIS — ONE GAL'S STORY
by Lia Bandola

I was born to immigrant Italian parents, and my first exposure to "networking" was nothing short of chaotic, fun, loud, lively, and always unpredictable. Gatherings with my extended family provided the perfect platform for learning how to "network." My role was clearly defined — I was the "good daughter" who did as she was told and wouldn't dare talk back to my parents or, for that matter, even express an opinion. Don't get me wrong: I loved my parents, and I know they were just doing what they thought good parents did, which was to raise us under strict rules and parameters. They were European, after all, and that was how you raised "good" kids — with a firm hand. And we are going back a lot of years, so in those days kids were treated like kids and not permitted to interact with adults in "grown-up" ways.

Early in life, I learned what I needed to do in the outside world to be heard and recognized, and set about developing my many other roles in life so that I would be important in some way and would leave a legacy of some kind. Along the way, I broke a few rules, rebelled against the "good girl" persona I had to put on for my parents, and established a great "friend role." I was loyal and trustworthy, and maybe willing to go along with more than I should have so that I would fit in with the crowd. It wasn't until much later in life that I started to explore who I really was, not who everyone else wanted me to be.

As my life progressed, I graduated from college and worked as a legal assistant before deciding to go back to school later in life to change careers and became a counsellor. I had many different careers, started several different businesses, was a wife, mother, writer, talk-show host, speaker, and so on. There was no shortage of roles and creative pursuits. There was never a dull moment, and there were many periods where day-to-day life was downright chaotic! The juggling sometimes was an act that I struggled to keep up. But I did, and made it through all the chaos. My kids grew up relatively unscathed, thankfully, and are fantastic adults, so I guess I did something right there! Oh, I guess my husband can have some of the credit, too.

Evolving Roles

THAT'S WHAT LIFE is really about — learning what our roles are and doing what we need to do to fulfill those roles. We spend our lives learning what we need to know to be "good" children, students, employees, spouses, friends, parents, and so on. And then we go about our days doing tasks and connecting with people on whatever level necessary to get the job — whatever that is — done. Sometimes our roles get tangled up with each other, and confusion can have us stepping outside of those roles. Sometimes we just want to run away from everything and live on a beach somewhere! This is typically the point where we need to take a step back and really take a long, hard look at our lives. We need to determine if we are living authentically or if we are just trying to keep everyone else around us happy. These identity crisis are typically the precursors to significant change needing to take place. They are our wake-up calls to shift to living from within our souls and to figure out what we are truly meant to do.

The problem is that life isn't nice and neat and tidy, and just when we think we've got a role or position down, life throws us a curveball and everything we thought we knew goes out the window. This is how the last two years of my life have felt — one big roller-coaster ride! There have been a lot of great moments and many very challenging moments too. My roles as I've known them have changed dramatically, and my confidence in myself and who I am has been shaken to the core.

Was the outside world aware of this "inner crisis" I was experiencing? No, I don't believe anyone was. I did a great job of hiding it, and just continued to go through my days doing what I needed to do to keep life humming along. Even though inside I felt like everything I knew was turned upside down, I just kept doing what I needed to do to get through my days without anyone being the wiser.

I've lost both of my parents: my father fifteen years ago, and my mother just a year and a half ago. So my greatest role in life (as a daughter) is now gone. I felt as though I was on a stage with no lines to say. That was a tough one to take. When you lose your parents, you feel like an orphan, no matter how old you are. My eldest son left home a year and a half ago, at the age of twenty-four — just two months before my mother passed away — and my youngest child went off to university this fall. My middle boy just turned twenty-three, and while he still technically lives at home, he is basically living his life independently. So my role as a mother has also taken quite a dramatic shift. I made a decision a year ago to close my practice as a counsellor, so that's yet another role that is gone. And my role as a wife also naturally transitioned because of all the other shifts I was going through. My position with Power of Women Exchange has become a full-time gig, and as POWE grows and expands, my role with it also escalates. As some roles go away and others change, we must learn new lines.

But what has all this role shifting and loss done to me as a woman? Well, it's sent me into a tailspin, questioning who I am and just what exactly my true purpose is in this world. It has affected how I relate to people, both on a personal level and in my business relationships. But I'm transcending the loss of my past roles and evolving and redefining who I am today and what my roles are now. And I know that the best is yet to come and new roles are forming all the time. The greatest shift for me is realizing that I am not my roles; I am who I am at my core. I bring to my roles everything I am as a woman in my own right. That empowering insight was difficult to arrive at, but has helped me define who I really am.

Define Who You Are

THE POINT OF my sharing this little part of my story is to illustrate that we often allow ourselves to be defined by what those around us say we should be. Depending on where you live and how you are raised, roles — even though the same on the surface — can be very different. Being a daughter or a parent can mean many things to many people in widely disparate parts of the world.

Sometimes, women are very comfortable with the clear-cut roles they have. Sometimes, there is confusion and a longing to have different roles. The stories you're about to read in this book show just how our experiences and upbringing can form who we are today. This, in turn, affects how we relate to people, how we do business, and how we live our lives in general.

This book comes at a time when more women than ever are entering the self-employment world. Our goal with Power of Women Exchange is to help women succeed in their business-building efforts and in their own journeys in life. This is also the same goal for anyone reading this book. We want to help women all over the world, from every walk of life, in every life circumstance, and of every race, to have the same opportunity at success, however they define success for themselves.

The tragedy is that there are still many women in the world who feel that success is out of their reach. We live in a world where pay equity for women is still not happening in many places, including Canada and the U.S. where one would expect enlightenment!

We live in a world where abused women feel they have no choice but to stay with their abusers because they can't pay for their own and their children's basic needs. We can change that! We live in a world where some places have women still completely relying on their men for survival — economically and otherwise. We can change that! We live in a world where many women are tortured and have unspeakable horrors happen to them simply because they are women. We can change that! We, as a collective, can change all of these travesties and so much more.

The Power of Women Exchange provides the platform for women to shine, have voices, and receive support, education, inspiration, and motivation, all of which can be shared by you and with you. Networking is really about relationship building or relational marketing — marketing your business or yourself through building relationships. We all have a story to tell, and this is part of mine — so far. I'm not done yet! This book is really about so much more than networking — it's a collection of stories told by amazing women who have been through many different challenges and experiences, and have defined their roles in life through those experiences. They are here to offer you what they've learned — what works and what doesn't work in life and in business. My wish is that you will be able to relate to some or all of these stories and that they will help you in the spinning of your own story.

About
Lia
Bandola

THE POWER OF Women Exchange is a unique organization that has tackled head-on the challenges of propelling women toward success in their chosen fields. As chief executive operating director of POWE, Lia Bandola is at the forefront of career issues facing women. From both personal and professional experience, she understands how to help women succeed.

A highly sought-after personal coach, counsellor, speaker, facilitator, writer, entrepreneur, and radio talk-show host, Lia personifies achievement. She is passionate about sharing her experiences and knowledge with others in an effort to help them live their best lives and to achieve harmony and balance both personally and professionally.

In addition to all of her other endeavours, Lia is the owner of Life Lessons Unlimited (winner of the 2004 Business of the Year Award), which specializes in personal coaching, workshops, "teleclasses," and public speaking engagements.

This busy wife and mother of three adult children also enjoys travel and several other creative pursuits, which she feels give her life much-needed balance.

Please visit Lia at
www.powe.ca
www.lifelessons.ca

Chapter 11

WHO AM I TO WIN BUSINESS
PERSON OF THE YEAR?
BY TINA DEZSI

Chapter 11

WHO AM I TO WIN BUSINESS PERSON OF THE YEAR?

by Tina Dezsi

From the beginning, I knew in my heart — I mean I really knew — I was meant for big things, and I say this with confidence and out loud! Like many of the authors in this book, I was afraid to let people know how I felt for fear of ridicule or, worse, them telling me it was just simply not true. (And by the way, even though in my heart I knew, my brain kept saying, "Yeah right, who do you think you are? What makes you think you are so special that you should stand out and achieve those 'over-the-top dreams and goals' you have?")

Part of me had no doubt, and yet the other part of my brain yelled back at me, *"Not you, Princess…you're not good enough, my dear!"*

Sound familiar? Come on, you know who you are — you ladies who can commiserate with me. Be truthful. I am sharing this with you, so be honest with yourself — *own it, sister!*

I was blessed to have parents who believed in my abilities and encouraged me — no, actually pushed me — to be great, to always do my best and then some, at everything I did. All the while making me strive for better; and this, of course, led me down the path to my perfectionist disorder. An "A" was not good enough when there was that elusive "A+" out there waiting for me to work a little harder.

Through the years, I stepped back and hid my thoughts. Here and now I can share this with you: I was terrified of my own potential. As crazy as that may sound to some who know me, you can believe it. I was terrified that I was great, that I knew I would accomplish extraordinary feats and inspire others to be the best they could be, yet I was scared to death to let people know of both my terror and my potential for greatness.

I put my tough exterior, my suit of armour, around myself to hide the fact that I knew my intelligence was immense, my ability to see a vision complete is one in a million, my intuition is very keen, and my tenacity is profound. I didn't want to scare people or, worse, scare myself. I was petrified to have people think I was full of myself, so I hid it away, turned the dimmer switch down on my light so that others could shine brighter. So you say, "Hey, Tina, this is what we are supposed to do."

Well, I beg to differ. *We must be the example of the change we want to see in the world, as Gandhi teaches us.*

Show Your True Greatness

LOOKING BACK, I believe I excelled at the times in my life when I truly did what I loved doing and didn't care what anyone thought about it or me. I showed the world my true greatness without reservations, and when I did that it always felt comfortable and right. Then my true self always felt right within itself, and I felt in line with "me" and proud of my accomplishments. The times when I was trying to live up to someone else's expectations of me and within the limits they put upon my abilities, I was miserable. I suppose I did okay, at least according to others' standards, but it was never great in my mind. I always felt "just not good enough" and would tell those others that it could have been better if I had done this or that.

I came to terms with my entrepreneurism at the very last job I will ever have, when I felt my spirit being broken, my confidence and self-esteem literally leaving my body at an alarming rate, all beyond my control. I knew I had to leave to save myself, my beautiful mind and my wonderful heart, or that giant person I was meant to be would be forever gone. I fled, I cried and I listened to my heart beating out of my chest, hearing my inner voice saying, "Tina, you must slow down and determine what it is that you need to be happy." Then it came to me in a flood of emotion mixed with enthusiasm, energy and terror: You must start your own business; you know this is where you are meant to be; you know you must share your gifts; *you* are obligated to help others; *you* must go forth and live your dream to change the world. *You* are truly meant for great things.

Being Tina can be difficult sometimes, as I have a tendency to jump into the deep end first and then look around for the ladder. Having that trait has led me down many paths of vulnerability that may have been avoided had I been more cautious. However, looking for the safe route may have also blocked me from travelling the road I did, missing out on a tremendous journey along the way. Has it been easy for me in my journey as an entrepreneur? Absolutely not. In fact, it has been the hardest thing I have ever done. I thought my path to freedom began the day I finished my first business plan. I am here to tell you that is simply not true; however, over the years with my many ups and downs (that is for another book), I have gained tremendous respect for all those who built businesses before me and a new-found respect for myself and my team. I have also learned that you must have fun every day, that there is no shame in hard work, and, yes, to expect greatness from yourself. There is no shame in shouting your vision and your accomplishments from the rooftops. This was the hardest thing I have ever done; however, it was definitely the most rewarding.

At this intersection of my journey, I now know this: By letting my light shine, by showing my gift of vision, by leading by example and letting others in on the secret that I am accomplishing great things, I share with them that they too can be all that OUT LOUD! We have an obligation to celebrate our gifts by sharing them with others. It is our own, the most precious thing we have been given, and we must pay it forward.

On this journey of mine, I have allowed myself to break promises to the most important person in my life, to sometimes treat her worse than I would treat an enemy, to talk her down, and to lie to her. She has been my biggest supporter and my worst critic. Today, I am able to say that I love her more then anyone in my life — she is me.

Your Opinion Is the Only One That Matters

WITHOUT TAKING THE time to allow myself healing, I believe I will not achieve my dreams. By listening to others' gossip, judgments, criticisms, or even their ideas of what I should do, I somehow allow that to pierce through my convictions, and then I somehow own it as a fact in my life. Coming to the realization that they are their opinions, most of the time born out of jealousy or their own lack of self-esteem (perhaps worrying I may be greater than them), I have a choice: to make them facts in my life or throw them away with yesterday's rubbish.

The greatest lesson this has taught me is that if I choose to own these opinions, I am the only one to blame, as I stay small inside my comfort zone. When I look back at the great big dreams not achieved, I truly have no one else to blame but myself. I have the choice to trust myself, trust my heart, and believe in my own abilities to achieve — to be successful at — whatever I choose to do. I am blessed to be able to reinvent myself and my dreams anytime I want. I am able to stretch beyond the self-imposed barriers I have put in place and dictate my own success beyond those self-reduced expectations. Setting goals too low serves only to accept mediocrity in our lives and shields us from our own disappointments in ourselves.

I have forgiven myself for all of this; I wiped my slate clean and now seek to gain knowledge and empowerment from others who have walked the journey before me. I look inside myself for the support, the truth to my own insecurities and the inspiration to go for my great big dreams. I not only listen now but also really hear the lessons that are put in front of me, and I will enjoy them for what they are: the good, the bad, and the ugly.

I truly believe that with the right combination of ammunition, power, and fuel we can all live the lives of our dreams, achieve those great big dreams, and be the best people we can be for ourselves. *The Power of Women United* is a momentous dream come true. In our effort to bring a book to the world that embraces the power of successful individual women and their collective awesomeness, we sought out the most *remarkable* women to share their stories of triumph in creating their own lives. These women are not famous celebrities; they are real women, like you, making their way along their journeys, ploughing the path for others who will come after them.

The twenty women in this book share intimate details of triumph through failure. They are truly women with visions, women who are shaping their own destinies and stories and are sharing their gifts with you, so that you may gain insight and knowledge to grow your own courage and confidence. Know that you are not alone as you learn from their paths and discoveries. Each of these beautiful women have made sacrifices and have risen from their own ashes to put into words lessons and wisdoms to offer you support as you take the next step in your own journey.

Whether you are a woman in transition trying to find out who you are, what your passions really are, and what your purpose is, or you are an entrepreneur looking for support and comfort in knowing you are not alone, this book is for you. This book speaks to women who are just starting their journeys as well as those stuck somewhere along the path trying to figure out what to do next. This is the true beauty of networking: As you build a relationship with each of the remarkable, memorable women in these pages, my hope for you is to become more of who you really are and share that greatness inside of you out loud!

Along the way, keep this book as a tool, a constant companion, and allow the words from these pages to speak to you often. Allow these women's words to mentor you and provide a light to brighten your path as you build your confidence, until you are ready to let your light shine! Someone once told me that you are never alone if you choose not to be, *so be bold*, and *mighty forces* will come to your aid.

This compilation of true empowerment is the mighty force — an army of strength — to help you conquer those big hills. Open your mind and your heart, and really hear the lessons on these pages. Break free of excuses, and finally take the reins and guide your own success!

About

Tina Dezsi

TINA DEZSI is an award-winning entrepreneur, speaker, visionary and the owner of her destiny. Recognition of her success includes The Phenomenal Woman 2008 Award and Business Person of 2008 for her area. Tina currently serves as president of T&E HealthPros Inc., a company she shares with her mother. Through this endeavour, they enjoy helping others live their lives with dignity and comfort. Tina is also a Canadian jewellery designer of her own collection — Jewelry by T.

Tina is a founder and CEO of Power of Women Exchange (POWE), an organization dedicated to bringing entrepreneurial women together to network and build their businesses. With her background in human resource management and more than thirty years of marketing and sales experience, she plans to make POWE the premier women's networking group for entrepreneurial women worldwide. Tina has published numerous articles and has developed a Marketing/Business Plan Program that she teaches to groups and individuals. Believing that giving is our key to freedom, she frequently volunteers for many non-profit organizations and participates in countless fundraisers. Sharing her knowledge and gifts, Tina mentors others to be the best they can be. Tina's commitment to inspire others to greatness is evident each and every day through her passionate engagement with each person she encounters.

Please visit Tina at
www.powe.ca
www.tnehealthpros.com

Chapter *III*

DOWN-TO-EARTH GIRL

BY DEBORAH VAN PELT

Chapter III

DOWN-TO-EARTH GIRL
by Deborah Van Pelt

Who couldn't use a bit of help, right? If none of us had ever received some form of guidance or help, where would we be? As a woman, my natural instinct is to nurture and care for others, so when asked to contribute in the writing of this book, I felt that it was perfectly aligned with who I am. I believe in helping one another, and that is really what networking is about, too. It isn't just about meeting people; it's about getting to know them and perhaps lending a hand for more than a handshake. Networking is about giving. I am a firm believer that when you're a good person, you share yourself, and if you truly want good things for others, you shall *receive*.

I hope that I can impart my own personal experiences and knowledge to give you a snapshot of my life and help you along your journey toward networking success. There are a few (if not most) of us who struggle with confidence now, or at least at some point in our lives, and have feelings about not belonging in these circles. Well, please get that thought out of your head *now!*

Networking is for everyone — you, too — and believe it or not, you will see after reading the stories in this book that most of you have already been using these skills. Relationship building with everyone you meet, and I mean *everyone,* is one of the most worthwhile skills you can possess when you really want to be a successful networker. I am contributing to this book merely to share with you, the woman or man who is starting out on your own journey and is wondering where to start and what to do. You'll find in this chapter my take on networking for beginners because I believe in simplicity and authenticity and, above all, just being you.

Before I continue, I would like for you to have a fairly good understanding of who I am and where I came from. After all, it's difficult to take advice from someone if you have no context, right? As far as early childhood…let's just say that I didn't have one, at least not one that you would recognize, and it is not something that I really want to discuss at length. To keep it simple and honest, I am quite grateful for the poverty, neglect, and abandonment I endured. Grateful, you ask? Yes, I really have to say I am grateful, because those early experiences shaped my mind and contributed to the person I am today. All of our experiences, the good and the bad, should be acknowledged and even embraced, not covered up or ignored, because those events and relationships make us unique.

My compassion, commitment, dedication, and work ethic were initially driven by having tasted the embarrassing effects of poverty. I wanted more. I am the second youngest of five children: four girls and a boy. My parents both worked very hard but were never home, and even when they were home on Sundays (a holiday in the late '60s), they spent their time drinking too much and engaging in their regular, ritual fight, and finally, when I was nine, my mother left my father, taking us away with her.

There was very little money for food or clothes, just the absolute minimum for necessities, and I was told many times, "You're lucky to have a roof over your head!" If things became any worse for us, she said, she would have to call the Children's Aid Society. Needless to say, I didn't complain. At the age of eleven, I began working, and although it was only babysitting for some children in my apartment building for fifty cents an hour, I considered it employment. I relied on my little income, as it provided me with the money I needed to buy clothes for school and personal items that my single mother could not afford. This was my first networking experience, and although I didn't use this term then, I began to meet women in the building, letting them know who I was and whom I had babysat for already, and asked each of them for a job or for referrals!

At thirteen, I lied about my age on a job application and said I was sixteen. I was hired and began working as a cashier in Kresge's Department Store after school and on weekends. I loved people, and I loved sales; it was fun to chat with customers and to see what things they bought. I took a personal interest in everyone I met, in what they wanted, and learned to provide good customer service, because when I did, I received several commendations. The store manager came to rely upon me and gave me more responsibility, making me feel important and grown up indeed!

At sixteen, I wanted to work and earn more money, although I really preferred to help my mother if I could. I obtained full-time employment and was offered a position with an excellent and reputable employer — Bell Canada — back in the early '70s. It was just before the workplace became too strict about university educational requirements for me to even be considered for a position. I had not completed my formal education, and I experienced my first taste of shame during the interview. I always felt that maybe I wasn't good enough.

I recall a particular human resources manager calling my mother. (Can you believe it — the employer calling to see if it was okay to hire me?) She carefully explained to my mother that this very reputable telecommunications company would provide all kinds of training and education opportunities for her sixteen-year-old daughter and felt that I would do extremely well with them. "Quite well," she said. She thought I was very mature. I would earn more income than my single mom and be able to contribute to the rent and food. It really wasn't something a teenager normally needed to think about in those days — school and poverty or money and a great job! As a result, I had a very successful career with Bell Canada for twenty-five years.

Networkquette

I WISH I'D had a book when I began to network to help me learn some basic "networkquette" (as I call it — my term for networking etiquette), and to help me fit in with this new circle of older women. The awkwardness most of us feel in new work and social situations is not unique to you; most people just don't talk about it. Well, I can tell you I sure was full of anxiety at first. But I still loved it! So please allow me to share some tidbits with you, hoping that I am a resource and helpful to you on your own journey. I have been there, so come along and follow me on the networking path.

In my earlier days of networking, I really wasn't sure what to do or even if I should be there at all. I lacked confidence and was intimidated by the many professionals around the room. I acted shyly, stood in the shadows and just listened, not really participating in the conversations very much at all. I wondered silently if that human resources manager had made a huge mistake. However, even when I was silent and merely observing, I was learning. I just wasn't sure what to do.

I wasn't a business owner or an executive, I was "just" a sales professional and would invariably show up late, just getting in under the wire, and look sheepishly around the room, afraid someone might see me and ask, "What is she doing here? She is nobody!"

A time came, however, when I realized that I did belong there too, and, more than anything else, this was the right place for a salesperson to be. It was ideal for anyone wanting to meet others and make connections. I must say, however, that getting to events and other opportunities but not taking advantage of the possibilities I encountered was one of the biggest learning curves earlier in my life. You see, EVERY interaction is an OPPORTUNITY.

Walking into a room and robotically handing out your business card just to "get it out there," without taking time to even get to know the person you're handing it to, is a big mistake and can be a costly one, too. Without establishing some kind of personal connection or rapport, most people you hand your card to will just file it away (or worse, toss it in the trash) with all the other cards they accumulated from people they don't know. Don't be that uncaring robot-person; be appropriate, be respectful, and build relationships, not just a card file!

Consistency is a strategy that works best for me in building relationships and getting to know people. I want to do business with others and act as a resource to help others. Listed below are a few networking tips that have helped me:

- I joined organizations that interested me and complemented what I do.
- I joined several women's networking groups because women are natural networkers.
- Early on, I joined my local chamber of commerce to meet like-minded business people.
- I wrote articles and newsletters and then submitted them to local papers to get my name out there.
- Magazines published articles I wrote that were appropriate for my work.
- I organized and promoted events such as luncheons, seminars, and social events.
- I visited churches, synagogues, mosques, and other cultural facilities.

- I made it a point to get to know people who work with me internally; this is networking also, as associates and employees all have families, churches, or organizations, and those can become extended contacts and possible friends!
- I attended fundraisers, festivals, interfaith meetings, and Iftars (breaking of the Muslim Ramadan fast).
- I organized clergy from local churches to attend a seminar by their peers dealing with their profession.
- I have always sought other areas of interest where large groups of people were likely to gather.
- I worked hard to piggyback onto other events and conferences.
- And finally, I attend tradeshows and set up booths to meet others at the show as well as other "boothers."

Thinking Outside the Box

AFTER RECEIVING SEVERAL awards for excellence in sales and customer service in the telecommunications industry, I felt it was time to try something new and enhance my resume, to make my mark in the world outside my comfort zone. I was anxious to try to help people and assist them in making changes that would enhance their lives. So, I enrolled at McMaster University in Hamilton, Ontario, in a program for addiction studies and counselling. After successfully graduating from that program and obtaining my diploma, a new journey awaited me.

Making a difference in some small way and helping people in the community became both my passion and my gift, and eventually evolved into a business plan and my becoming the owner and founder of Today's Gifts Resource & Wellness Centre. I am extremely proud of the work the Centre has accomplished.

My Centre was initially a self-help bookstore and conference centre, and it had a database for a speakers bureau, which I developed as a resource in my region for self-improvement and self-help initiatives.

My strength in networking began to shine during the process of owning and operating my own business. I began attending events in my area that not only interested me, but that I knew would also complement or benefit my business. I took a genuine interest in people, who they were, and what they did. Another beneficial decision was to join local community groups and health councils related to mental health, as well as sitting in on as many subcommittees as I could possibly manage.

To make my presence more visible, I volunteered at social events, introducing myself to everyone. I became a board member and got involved in community advocacy groups that aligned with my values on health and prevention issues, and as a result received two community awards for making a difference in the health of citizens in my community. I also took an interest in the people who hosted the many health-related workshops at my centre. I wanted to get to know them better and learn about their products and services, as well as help them gain better visibility and more clients for their workshops. This was a win-win situation.

I later decided to host a Health & Wellness Fair, where all of my alternative health care providers could educate the public and provide free services for the day. We met to plan, discuss advertising and promotional opportunities, and get to know one another. In the process, I was helping them grow their businesses. It was networking at its finest. Giving! You should never expect to "get" when joining a networking group; instead, just try giving first, and you will be amazed at how abundantly the rest will follow.

Dressing for Success

THIS TOPIC ALONE could fill its own book. It is a huge topic and deserves your thought and consideration. Think about those who grab your attention. Doom, gloom, and dowdy outfits or personality plus — colourful, stylish, and dressed for success? A person who is fun, friendly, outgoing, and kind is interested in what I say; they listen and converse back. If they have lots of humour, I gravitate towards them. Don't you? I had admired others and wanted to learn and to emulate some of that. Tsufit, a Bay Street lawyer in one of my networking circles turned actress and business coach, comes immediately to mind here for me. She lights up any room she enters with her exuberant, friendly manner and shares freely her true self with others. She always dresses cheerfully and therefore is dressed for success.

One of the most important tips I can offer you is to take a moment to think about the business impression you want to impart and leave with others — those with whom you wish to build relationships and do business. How do you want people to see you? How do you want them to remember and think about you? What image do you wish to project with your clothing and your demeanour?

One of the biggest mistakes I see happening today is that some people don't give this much attention, and it is critically important to your professionalism.

Investing in a business outfit that is both appropriate and efficient for your work is one of the best investments in yourself you can make. Make sure you are always well-groomed and tidy; your appearance is the first impression you leave with someone, so let it be a good one. Think about it!

When you attend an event, are you tidy, professionally attired and well-groomed? I ask this because, trust me, it is not unusual to be at a business networking luncheon and see a number of people in the group who look as if they dressed for a picnic at the beach. (This is appropriate only if it were a networking picnic.)

It is all about being appropriate — for the weather, the event, the attendees, and your profession. Putting together your "professional image" need not be an expensive venture; it can actually be done quite modestly. Observe the people in your networking room — the ones with the most influence. What are they wearing? How are they groomed? What is your perception? Are they dressed to impress? Now, take another look around the room at the ones who are "dressed down." Make a point to talk to both of these groups of people. Ask what they do, and note how they interact and respond to you and others. Which group do you want to belong to?

Until We Meet Again

I HOPE YOU have found this bit of sharing and information useful and helpful. I would love to one day meet you in one of my circles of networkers, whether in person, through a book, in the grocery store, at the hairdresser, at one of your children's school events, at a seminar, at a continuing education course, at a volunteer activity, or on the Internet — the possibilities are absolutely endless. Networking is everywhere, as is building relationships! Each and every relationship one builds through networking is a building block that will make one's life, business, or other endeavour grow and strengthen.

So, until we meet, may God bless.

About Deborah Van Pelt

AFTER HAVING COMPLETED a twenty-five-year career with Bell Canada, Deborah Van Pelt's training and background includes a diploma in addiction counselling from McMaster University, as well as being the founder and previous business owner of Today's Gift Resource & Wellness Centre.

Deborah began working as a preplanning advisor with the Mount Pleasant Group of Cemeteries in 2000 as her second career, shortly after the death of a loved one inspired her to do so. As an experienced licensed preplanning director, Deborah understands the unique needs of her clients and treats each individual and their family with personal attention and assistance.

Deborah enjoys helping others and finds many personal rewards in her career. It is her caring, compassionate manner in helping individuals and their families with this very important planning in their lives that she finds particularly rewarding.

Please visit Deborah at
www.deborahvanpelt.com

Chapter IV

LIFE IS SPEAKING;
ARE YOU LISTENING?
BY STEFANIE ANTUNES

Chapter IV

LIFE IS SPEAKING; ARE YOU LISTENING?
by Stefanie Antunes

"The greatest danger in life lies not in setting our aim too high and missing our mark, but aiming too low and achieving it."
— Michelangelo Buonarroti

All my life, I've been a dreamer. Most of us start out in life as dreamers, but somewhere along the way we become more conservative — more limited in our aspirations — what many people call "realistic" or "responsible." I was fortunate enough to grow up in a family where my parents told me that I could be whatever I wanted. I took that liberty to heart!

My mother was strong and raised my sisters and me to be confident, independent women. My father was also very loving and a great man. My childhood was a blessing that had a positive impact on me. While most people conformed to preconceived notions in early adulthood, I continued to dream like a little kid.

I remember my mother once calling me impetuous. At the time, I laughed and asked what that big word meant. If you look to the dictionary for a definition, you'll find that it means "characterized by a sudden or rash action or emotion; impulsive." I never truly understood why she considered it to be a negative label. From the time I was a young girl, I sensed that life was much too short to wait for the perfect time to do what we want, to wait for the perfect financial situation to have fun, to wait for the right time to be a little less "responsible." There was no way I was going to live my life in this manner.

At the age of fourteen, I told my parents that I wanted to tour Europe after high school. My parents were hesitant. They worried about me not returning to finish university, which was essential for success in their eyes. So I negotiated that if I could manage to finish high school a year early, then they should let me go. I used the rationale that I'd be starting university at the same age as all my friends anyway. They finally agreed, probably thinking it was a feat of gigantic proportions, one which I was unlikely to accomplish. Boy, were they in for a surprise! I took both summer and night classes in every grade in order to finish a year early. To hold up their end of the bargain, my parents reluctantly let me go to Europe. I spent an amazing year abroad, which changed me forever. Even at that young age, I realized that to be successful I needed to have a vision, a mission, a goal, and I needed to map out the steps to reach my desired destination. As the saying goes: "If you don't know where you're going, any road will get you there."

There Is No Time Like the Present

ONE TIME, I watched a great demonstration involving pencil and string, and I've incorporated it into as many of my own speaking engagements as possible. First, I place a string or piece of paper on the ground and ask for a volunteer to jump over it. After each jump, I then move the object farther from the starting point. Each time, the person jumps farther and farther, until they reach a point where they say, "I don't think I'll be able to jump that." With a little encouragement from the audience and me, they're able to jump successfully every time.

With the string or piece of paper only a foot away from them, no one ever jumps as far as they are able, because that is not their goal. This exercise helps them to realize that the bigger the goal, the farther they jump. As T.S. Eliot said, "Only those who will risk going too far can possibly find out how far one can go."

I've never lacked the tenacity needed to act on my dreams. The truth is, to me it was far worse not to have a dream: to live a life with no goals, vision, or purpose. Perhaps you hate your job and think there is no way out or that you don't have the luxury to quit and follow your dream. The truth is, you don't have the luxury not to! While you sit at a job you loathe, or on a couch watching TV all day, life is passing you by. It waits for no one. Life doesn't wait for your finances to be in order, for your kids to be the "right" age, or for your partner to support you. In fact, life won't send you what you need until you're ready to take a leap of faith and grab it.

The universe (God) wants and needs you to dream. For life to flow correctly and everything to fall into place, you need to find your reason for being here. What were you put here to accomplish? And lest you think you are some rarer-than-rare exception, know that we all have a purpose. Your children need to see you pursue your dreams so they can one day do the same. When all is said and done in your life, don't let your biggest regret be the realization that you were too afraid, too "conservative," too responsible to dream and venture into the wild unknown.

Leaps of Faith

I SPENT THE better part of a decade trying to discover my life's mission. I watched television shows, read books, and listened to speakers, all the while feeling frustrated, lost, and disillusioned. I knew I was put here to do something great, but I couldn't for the life of me find what it was. That is, until I started taking little leaps of faith. We're all afraid to take those leaps of faith, and have many excuses why we shouldn't. But courage has nothing to do with the absence of fear; rather, it's forging through that fear to get to your goal.

Like many women, I was a working mom, trying to be a success in my career and making small advancements to receive small pay raises so that I could buy more "stuff." I had a son from my first marriage and was struggling with work/life balance. I didn't work super-long hours (I did put my foot down there), but by the time I added on the commute time, my son was in daycare for ten to eleven hours a day. None of it felt right. I wanted the career, but I hated the seemingly wasted hours of the commute. If I chose to work locally (instead of commuting), I was looking at a significant pay decrease. My excuses were plentiful. Then life sent me a whispered message, and I had a pivotal moment.

I was reassigned to a new boss who had just joined the company. In an effort to get to know her staff, she invited us all individually to lunch. At our one-on-one lunch, she asked me what I wanted out of my life. I told her how much I was enjoying the corporate world and saw myself in increasingly senior roles. She then told me that in life we have to choose between being a mom and having a career. (Obviously, she had decided not to have children.)

Taken aback at first, I sheepishly said that I had always thought we could have both. Looking back now, I can see that her life was filled with "stuff." The materialistic things she had were used to fill the void left by her egotistical and — I believe — selfish ways. After our conversation, I took a week off and flew halfway around the world to be by myself and think long and hard about what I truly wanted out of life. After returning from my trip, I quit. I had no other job prospects, but I knew that was **not** an environment conducive to the elusive work/life balance I desired. Talk about a leap of faith!

But I was an avid go-getter with numerous skills and talents, and I was eager to learn all sorts of new subject matter. It didn't take me long to find another job. A couple of years later, after having my second son, I decided after maternity leave that the corporate world wasn't for me. So I took another leap of faith and decided to start my own business. I knew very little about writing a business plan, setting up a website, using accounting software, doing business taxes, or invoicing. It was all new. I felt excited and overwhelmed at the same time.

Like everyone else who starts their own business, I worried about the financial impact on my family if matters didn't go well. Instead of worrying about the "what ifs" (which we are all very aware of), I decided to focus on my business and envision myself as a success. Then I acknowledged what I didn't know, which was virtually everything, and I learned it very quickly.

I focused on one main principle: Just because we are a small business, it doesn't mean we have to look like a small business.

The key thing to be aware of is that we can't do it all, and we need to align ourselves with people who can help, just like the world's biggest CEOs do. They delegate, and so should small business owners. We need to follow that up with a healthy leap of faith and accept opportunities that present themselves to us that are in line with our mission and goals. I believe life whispers answers to us, but, unfortunately, most of us ignore this quiet voice.

Many people claim they can't hear these messages. The problem is that often times we don't want to hear them. We fill our lives with "noise" and ignore the important messages sent our way. What if your message says, "Quit your job," "Go back to school," or "Put your foot down"? They all require leaps of faith and can cause great turmoil in your life. When we truly open ourselves up to these messages, we do hear them — loud and clear.

Unfortunately, without taking that leap of faith, you will never know the amazing life that awaits you on the other side of those tough choices. If I hadn't listened, I wouldn't have the pleasure of sharing my story with you.

Life forces us into those choices anyway, but then it becomes on life's terms, not ours. I see people who heard the early whispered warnings but chose not to listen. They may fall ill from stress and be forced to quit their jobs. They may get fired and have to go back to school, or their partners may leave them and increase the negative impact in their lives. You choose your life, or life will choose it for you.

Until I learned this lesson, life chose a bumpy path for me. Around the time I opened my first business, another opportunity presented itself. My first childbirth was a dreadful ordeal. Not that anything really bad happened, but it wasn't the empowering experience I'd hoped for. After having taken Lamaze® classes during my second pregnancy, the experience was wonderful and I wanted to share this with other parents so that they could avoid the kind of first encounter I had. As a result, I became a Lamaze® educator and a doula, and those jobs took hold of my heart…and my life.

I now realize that we can't search for our mission, and I often work with people to help them understand this as well. Instead, we need to open our hearts, our inner-ear intuition, and our world to what life/God has in store for us. Only when we do this — and truly mean it — will life send us the right people at the right time, and the right opportunities for us to uncover life's most coveted secret — our life's purpose. Everything will begin to fall into place. As the old saying goes, "Synchronicity is God's way of remaining anonymous." The rest is up to us.

If we pray for patience, we won't be given patience, but the opportunity to learn it. If we pray for our mission, it won't knock at our door one day with a package to be signed for; it will come to us in small opportunities. If we ignore enough of these opportunities, life will begin sending us lessons until we do listen. These lessons become increasingly uncomfortable as we ignore them. An analogy I like to use: Life starts by sending us a stubbed toe. If we ignore it, we find ourselves with a skinned knee, then a tumble and a bruised behind (and ego), then a bloody nose, and then we get hit by the proverbial "Mack truck" of life lessons.

Many times, I hear people say, "I just can't get a break," or "Bad things seem to follow me around," or "I just have the worst luck." I smile because I know the answer lies in one of two possibilities: Either people are not learning the lessons from the negative experiences sent to them or they are completely ignoring the early warning messages (whispers) sent to them. I now prefer to listen at the stubbed-toe stage, and my friends and family will often see me, arms in the air, saying, "I'm listening. You can stop. I'm all ears!"

The Correct Path

LIFE HAS MANY paths. At any moment, we are just minutes away from a transformative experience that is as yet unbeknown to us. These experiences can be good or bad, but they will transform us in the way we allow them to. I now spend my life working to help new parents have transformative childbirth experiences. This one moment in life is either exhilarating or destructive, and it marks us as we enter parenthood. Most women don't realize just how much this one moment impacts them. Some of it is psychological, and much of it is biological: a beautiful cocktail of hormones that can catapult us into the bliss of motherhood, but only if we allow it to happen in a certain way.

I often speak with my clients about their goals. As a doula, it's my role to help show them the path that is most likely to lead them to their goals. Sometimes we're tempted to take a path that seems clear and safe, but it can be an illusionary path, filled with large potholes that we don't see until we're too far down the path to turn back. Sometimes the path that leads us to our goals appears uneven and bumpy, but after only a short while, it becomes the most beautiful ride of our lives, with the most magical, breathtaking scenery. The initial sight of the bumpy, uneven path leads most of us to avoid it altogether. What a loss! Sometimes getting over the bumps (challenges) takes us around the corner to our dreams.

The more time I spend committed to my life's mission, the more wonderful my life becomes. You'll know when you've found your real life purpose, because it will have at its core an element of helping others. There would be no greater world than one where we were all focused on selfless life missions. Now, don't get me wrong: When I say selfless, I don't mean of Mother Theresa proportions here. Having nice things and making money at our mission is great, and most of us find that if we're on the right track, this flows to us quite naturally. An important aspect to remember is that life isn't about accumulating "stuff." People who live with this philosophy will never feel full; they will always hunger for the next thing because all materialistic people feel a constant void. They seek to fill that void, however, with things that are as insubstantial as air.

I would like to say that my life has been free from problems. Quite the contrary. Many times, I've ignored the early warnings (whispers) and run into the Mack truck–sized life lessons. I prefer, however, to look at the amazing lessons I've learned through those tumultuous times. Although some of those circumstances — most profoundly my divorce — were some of the worst moments of my life, I acknowledge them as the best events to have happened to me, because of the personal growth I experienced as a result. I'm excited about what else life has to send my way, and I think I'll try as much as possible to learn at the stubbed-toe or skinned-knee stage!

Gratitude for what we already have — our gifts, our talents, our families and friends — brings even more wonderful things into our lives. I feel truly grateful for the amazing people in my life who surround me with friendship beyond what anyone could ask for, and for a partner who is more supportive than is imaginable.

I urge you not to waste one more minute waiting for the "right" time. Live your best life every day. Live the life you were put here for: Your authentic life. Let the world be a better place because you're here. Say these words to yourself every single day: "The world is a better place because I'm here."

If you don't believe them now, then do something, and do it fast. Act on your dreams, because if you don't act on life, life will act on you.

"The World is a great book, of which they who never stir from home read only a page."
— St. Augustine

*About
Stefanie
Antunes*

STEFANIE ANTUNES is a Lamaze Certified Childbirth Educator and certified doula with DONA. As owner of Discover Birth, she helps expectant parents prepare for childbirth in a fun and positive way. She attends births with couples so they can fully experience the amazing potential of this transformative event.

Stefanie, a mother of three, is an advocate in the childbirth movement, helping to decrease maternal and infant mortality rates across North America through the awareness of safe practices and an evidence-based approach. She helps other doulas and childbirth educators run their businesses successfully by having them join the Discover Birth team, allowing them to focus on affecting change in their local communities.

Stefanie's previous corporate experience includes helping large organizations form appropriate strategies by researching and understanding their markets, their competitors, and their own strengths and weaknesses.

*Please visit Stefanie at
www.discoverbirth.com*

Chapter V

BABY STEPS TO PERSONAL
POWER AND SUCCESS
BY DARCELLE RUNCIMAN

Chapter V

BABY STEPS TO PERSONAL
POWER AND SUCCESS
by Darcelle Runciman

"Life loves to be taken by the lapel and told, 'I'm with you kid. Let's go."
— Maya Angelou

Much of my youth was spent unlike most others — just trying to figure life out and have fun along the way! I was, like most youngsters, focused on myself without giving much thought to how important relationships with others would become.

Networking and meeting people have helped me gain confidence in myself; I have met hundreds of great people, my work has been featured in real estate instructional manuals, and it has enabled me to meet great people who have since become joint venture owners on investment real estate.

I've learned that relationships are essential to all businesses. I've admired and gained much support from my mentors' valuable advice. They are extremely successful people, and the one common theme among them (my mentors) is their ability to speak from the heart. There is a significant difference between being taught a subject and having a mentor, and they are true mentors with the ability to lead by example. I owe them a tremendous debt of gratitude for helping me move forward along my path of personal growth.

"The biggest adventure you can take is to live the life of your dreams."
— Oprah Winfrey

IT'S OKAY…GOOD…great…and, yes, even necessary to believe in yourself, so that your mind and heart are open to the wonderful creation of success that resides within you. I believe we create our own success, and it is helped out along the way by the relationships we build around us. Allowing ourselves to be open to change and loving yourself first is how to find success. I am not talking about conceit, but a very quiet, confident, comfortable place within yourself where your spirit resides.

Even growing up I believed this, and now turning forty I am at that place where I understand how important knowing yourself and being "still" can be for the mind. As a real estate investor and business owner, life can get really crazy fast! Balance has been a key factor for me in ensuring sanity. Networking has also made many contributions to my life by giving me opportunities to meet with likeminded people who share my investing passion. I have met people with whom I have later become a joint partner, and it has brought me great friendships that have helped me develop and grow as a person.

Being true to yourself means recognizing what you want for yourself and having the persistence to follow through. We all have dreams. Many of us, however, are unsure how to motivate ourselves to do what it takes to make them come true. Years ago, a friend of mine and I completed many small cards that listed items that we loved to do for ourselves and called it our "personal gift" to ourselves. We wrote up about fifteen of our favourite activities and placed them in a shell container. Then, if at some point we realized that we needed time for ourselves in our busy lives, we were to open it up and do what the card said. Well, my friend passed away a few years ago, and every now and again I get a great reminder of that special friendship when I pull out one of my cards that tell me to call my friend Irene. Celebrate your successes. Value life, live in the moment, and cherish your family. You can bring more to the table if you value yourself first.

Success is a frame of mind. The power of your words, thoughts, and actions create your results. The words you use every day are powerful. Remember that your words are helping create not only how you see yourself but also how others see you. You need to have confidence, believe in yourself, and feel good about who you are as a person. It's very important that you make sure you're clear as to what it is that you want, so that you get the proper results. In other words, be careful what you wish for, and be specific. If you can visualize your goal, tell people you know and trust to be supportive and work hard to make it happen, and then success will follow.

The Power of Networking

suggested five-step process to networking success:

1. Get involved with groups — social, religious, professional, or civic.
2. Begin to let others know what you do.
3. Have something to offer the other person — communication is a two-way street.
4. Make the connection and then follow through.
5. Share in the process.

Networking, if done correctly, is much more than just letting someone learn what you do and exchanging business cards. It can be the catalyst to new adventures, more business, higher learning, and, best of all, a whole lot of fun! How have I networked to achieve my success? I am a member of a real estate networking group, part of POWE, and an active member of other women's groups. You need to recognize your power and…

- Realize it's all within you.
- Heal yourself first.
- Ask yourself what you can do to build your business.
- Talk to more people.
- Get "out there" on a regular basis.
- Join more groups, and get involved with your community.
- Pick a charity that speaks to your heart, and take action to support it.

Whether you are just starting out or have been in the game for many years, the Internet is a great place to start to find local groups in your area. Your local chamber of commerce can be another great resource, and they often have regular networking sessions that are free of charge. When I started out wanting to learn more about Canadian real estate content, I researched until I found a networking group that fit the bill.

Even before that, I was looking for a local group and found a small women's group to join; from there, I met Donna Messer, who I call a networking guru. I recommend you visit her site: www.connectuscanada. com.

She offered me a good deal of great training and support, and started me on my quest to get out there and to forget about my shyness and fears of speaking in front of people. Taking bits and pieces of experience from everyone you meet and learning from them can help you on your road to success, but don't forget to share in return.

My real estate investing success has been largely due to my relationships with people and having a proper system. Picking the right area is key, and ensuring that the numbers work. Projecting out to ensure we see the end result and not just jumping into a property is vital in investing. Once we can show them, our partners see and understand what it is we do and know they are in control of their destinies. Without the relationships built through networking and being out there, properties would not be bought and sold and many opportunities would be missed. Real estate gives me the freedom I choose now, while also taking care of the future. It's a fascinating and rewarding field in which the key to success hinges upon networking, building trust and credibility, and relationship building.

Listed below are some helpful hints you can use for any industry:
- Meet with joint ventures or potential clients:
  - Find those who have a shared vision or goal with you.
  - Learn about their focus and understand their financial goals.
  - Then do a risk assessment — ask questions, read the person, know your audience.
- Love what you do — watch for non-verbal cues:
  - Enjoying what you do comes across in your demeanour.
  - Your excitement for your passion is contagious.
  - Then become an expert to build credibility.
- Help other businesses become stronger:
  - If they want to learn and do it themselves, demonstrate how you can help them.
  - Utilize collaborative businesses — working towards a common goal.
- Asking the right questions at the right time — win-win:
  - What will help the other person — cash flow or appreciation, for example?
  - Learn what's important to them.
  - What are their needs? Do they need to obtain a financial overview first?

- Ask, "How can I help you?" Determine what they want to achieve.
- Ask for what you want — ask for referrals.

The Philosophy of Win-Win

THE COLLECTIVE, AT times, can achieve more than the individual. It's a fairly easy concept to grasp, but only if you truly believe in win-win — something for everyone. I learned long ago in business that you can have success; however, you *really* gain by creating a win-win situation for all parties involved. Networking works the same way; you are working towards a win-win for the collective. It's not so much about what you can get out of it; it's about what you can help create. How you help to construct a vast network of creative minds to achieve business goals is the ideal.

There have been many leaders that have assisted me over the years. Some that come to my mind are my mentor, Philip McKernan; Donna Messer, the guru of networking; and Don R. Campbell. These are the people I look up to and who have taught me that the whole can be greater than the sum of its parts.

Networking is a key ingredient to a person's success. It is all in what you can bring to the table, not simply what you can consume that others provide. How you help others succeed to achieve their goals will in the end help you grow as a person. Want to enhance your life, your business, your spirit? Read, network, be seen, listen to people, care about others, and share yourself.

"Follow your instincts. That's where true wisdom manifests itself."
— Oprah Winfrey

Strengths and Weaknesses

TOO OFTEN, WE as people, or perhaps as members of a Western society, focus on our weaknesses instead of our strengths. Working at what we love and are best suited for is not just for the lucky. People like Oprah Winfrey, Donald Trump, Tiger Woods, and Denzel Washington are successful not by chance or due to luck, but because they, like many others, have focused on what they are best at and then developed that craft. Tiger Woods didn't become perhaps the world's greatest golfer by luck. He had a natural talent, yes, but he spent countless hours on the golf course. He also listened to coaches and mentors throughout his life. He didn't achieve success alone or in a vacuum.

Concentrating on our strengths also helps us feel better about ourselves, which in turn helps our confidence, which helps how we project ourselves when we are networking. So understanding our strengths is extremely important. The best, most successful minds in business and in life know this. Your instincts show you your strengths and your brilliance if you listen, which in turn lead you to your correct path to understanding where you will excel and succeed. The way to do this is to have quiet time, time to be at peace. I enjoy hiking and being outside, and this is one way that I experience the world.

I made a decision some time ago that what I was doing was helping me achieve my goals in business, but in spite of financial rewards, my spirit was not being nourished. During that time I realized that my strengths were actually what I loved to do, which is business and real estate investing. So I decided that no matter what, I could do both. So that is what I have done.

Over the last few years, I have also realized the need to let go of the labels and attachments to my story or memories. In particular, to the one regarding the time it took to sell our business. You see, by my holding on to this, I was allowing the negativity to remain in my life. It wasn't until I began to learn how to release it mentally, believe that it would all be okay to let go, that it finally happened.

I know for sure it is possible for everyone to achieve what they want in life. It requires getting out of your own head and changing the way you think. Becoming a deliberate creator of what it is you want to be *or, better yet, just "being."* You can read about it, you can watch it in a movie, and you can even want it desperately, but until you learn that your lack of confidence and openness to the process is what holds you back, you may, just as I did, remain holding on to something that is holding you back.

When we realize that it is all up to us and that we have the ability to heal ourselves, true change begins. Once you do that, you undoubtedly heal all the relationships around you, including your work life and your family life. Isn't that what we really want? What I know for sure is that's exactly what I want. Knowing that and taking responsibility to be at peace with yourself will help you do just that. So get out there, have confidence in yourself, and get networking towards a more prosperous and rewarding business, a better life, and a better you.

Giving Back

FOR YEARS, IN fact since I was a teenager, I wanted to sponsor a child from World Vision. As the years passed and life threw its inevitable curveballs along the way, I did not follow through to make the commitment of sponsoring a child. Then finally, last year, I decided it was time to make our dedication to charities in a more personal way. Pat, my husband and business partner, and I decided to sponsor a five-year-old girl from Africa. I have been very proud of this achievement and commitment to be able to help even just one child. My charities of choice are Habitat for Humanity, helping families from Africa, World Vision, Kids Help Phone, and the SickKids Foundation. You will have your own special contribution interests, but I wanted to share my focus with you.

Systems, relationships, and following through on commitments and goals take time, but you never know where things will lead. I have had mentors who, years later, were able to do business with us because of the relationships developed through networking. Because of our shared belief in creating a win-win situation, we have brought forth a shared successful project. Real estate and business mentoring to me is a great way to fulfill my love for research, organization, and meeting people — all while creating income for now and in the future. Networking and the collective is a large part of our success. We have a team behind our company for research, legal and accounting, property management, and acquisition specialists. I believe anyone has the power to achieve success; you just have to really want it.

It's not about what you can do all on your own. It's about what you can achieve collectively, with others. Discovering your brilliance is what also contributes to your success. Discover what you love to do, what you are good at, and what comes to you easily. Doing that (identifying your strengths) and hiring out the rest of the tasks will truly make you successful. Being firm but fair, strong but loving, and successful but humble leads down Destination Success Road.

Hope to see you there!

About Darcelle Runciman

DARCELLE RUNCIMAN is a business mentor and real estate investor whose expertise is business development, company organization, project management, and marketing your business. Along with her passion for real estate, she enjoys mentoring business owners and entrepreneurs to recognize their strengths and inspire them to take action steps toward their dreams and to realize their financial goals.

Her career began with a degree in criminology and sociology and working on projects with various police agencies for the federal government and immigrant services, and she has an innate ability to work with people in any industry. Presently, Darcelle's marketing work has been produced in a collaborative training seminar regarding joint venture partners in the real estate investing field. Her work on diversity and the community has been used by local police agencies.

Darcelle has volunteered on boards and in various organizations such as the Quinte United Immigrant Services, Ottawa Police Community Policing, and Quinte Interfaith Refugee Sponsorship Committee. Currently, she is working on a Twelve Tips marketing product for real estate investors and entrepreneurs.

Visit Darcelle at
www.darcellerunciman.com and www.hemlockinvestments.ca

Chapter VI

PUT YOUR MIND TO IT

BY COREY MCCUSKER

Chapter VI

PUT YOUR MIND TO IT

by Corey McCusker

I'd like to dedicate this chapter to my mom. She was brilliant; in fact, she was a great businesswoman, brilliant communicator, and nurturing mother. My mother was passionate about a few things — her kids, hockey, and her work. Without those three things, she didn't feel alive. I'm grateful to her for what she taught me about believing in myself, connecting with others, and just going for it.

As a single mother, many times she worked two jobs to provide us with the best life possible. She enjoyed her business, thrived in her work, networked easily, and was able to get most jobs she went for. She'd have one job after another, always looking for more of a challenge, all the while believing in herself, which was evident in the confidence she exuded.

My first memory of her working was in the banking industry. She was one of the first women selected for the management program. At that time, banking was a man's world and she was trying to break into the field. Frustrated with the politics and the exclusivity of the men, she moved on, but she wasn't about to take no for an answer. My mom took action and went for many different opportunities, but not everything went her way and obstacles arose. Both my parents strongly believed that everything happens for a reason, and if it doesn't work out, it wasn't meant to be. A better opportunity is around the corner. I live by this credo today.

Sometimes that thinking isn't easy, but when I look back at how my life has unfolded, I realize this is true; there is always an abundance of opportunities, no matter how bleak the outlook appears. My most difficult challenges brought me my greatest opportunities and growth. As the saying goes, "When one door closes, another door opens." Or, "If you first don't succeed, try, try again." Those expressions have become cliché, but they are so true!

Sadly, at the age of forty-three, my mom died of a heart attack. Twenty-one at the time, I had a gut feeling that we were going to lose her. You see, my brother, Gord, and I were all grown up: We'd both started working, he'd stopped playing hockey, and we were both busy with our own lives. And after one of her attacks, the doctors said she could never work full-time again. In her mind, everything she loved was gone: her kids, hockey, and work. I believe this was the last straw. Her heart was empty, she felt alone, and her will to live was gone. Without work and her kids, she was lost. She was a woman with strong values and was passionate about life. When what you value in life is not being met, it has an impact on you.

Take Action and Responsibility

IF YOU WANT something, make a plan, take action, and go for it. My mom taught me this, especially when I was twelve. I desperately wanted a pair of jeans and asked her to buy them for me.

She said, "If you want the pair of jeans, buy them yourself. I can't afford to buy you jeans." I knew cash was tight, so I thought about it after having a bit of a temper tantrum. I was determined to have those jeans so I could be like the cool kids. I took action by asking around to see who needed a babysitter. I worked and saved up enough money to buy those jeans. That was the start of my working career, and from the age of twelve onward, I always had a job. I loved making money and having responsibility, and I thrived at it just like my mom always had.

I followed in my mom's footsteps and entered the banking industry. The only difference between her situation and mine was that I released the belief that this was a man's career, and I stayed in that field for twenty-one years. I knew I could climb the corporate ladder, all the way to the top. Limiting beliefs can prevent people from moving forward, and I wasn't going to allow that. My banking career began right out of high school, and I believed in myself and gave it my all from the first day. I had the right attitude — thank goodness! My positive attitude and drive to succeed have always presented me with great opportunities.

My first job in the bank was as a teller. I was great at serving clients and meeting their needs, but I could not balance my cash drawer at the end of the day. I always took full responsibility if I made a mistake and didn't balance, but I was determined to find out why this was happening and fix it. I always stayed in the bank until the error was found. Sometimes it was two or three hours after my shift had ended. This leads me to another important rule of business: Take ownership if you make mistakes or when errors happen, whether it is with clients, co-workers or anything else. Acknowledge it and own it. Never shrug and walk away. Never blame others. No one intentionally makes mistakes and wants to do a bad job; there is always a reason for it. My positive, optimistic attitude got me promoted quickly, and my experiences provided me with the foundation to help others.

Control Your Thoughts

MISTAKES OR CERTAIN events, circumstances, or situations happen for a reason, and maybe there is a lesson to learn, or it's not the right connection and a new opportunity could be around the corner. Many people react badly when things don't go their way, which is normal. People feel anger, hurt, upset, and rejection, and sometimes rush to blame others. Our minds control so much, and if we learn to control our minds and stay focused, we can control our world. Your Mind Matters is the name of my company! We choose our thoughts and therefore can be happy, mad, or sad, but the choice is ours.

My thoughts were always, "I can do it if I put my mind to it. I know I can." I remember my father saying to my bosses when he'd meet me for our regular weekly lunch date, "Corey thinks she's the president of the company." I liked to believe I was important and in charge, just like my mom reflected when she worked. My family believed in me and supported me in all that I did, especially my dad. That was important to me after I lost my mom. I didn't spend much time with him growing up, so having his support and knowing he believed in me was precious.

Promoted to management in my early twenties, I knew this was what I wanted to do — manage, empower, help people, and be a leader. I loved the responsibility, the diversity, and the multitude of tasks. I realized the importance of understanding people and effectively communicating with them. I had to build my client base by getting out there and networking, which felt natural. Networking to me was not only getting out and making connections and bringing in business, but it was also about building a network with my team and within the company. I needed to manage, motivate, and earn my team's respect as well as that of my superiors. The first step to accomplish this was to understand those around me — my staff, the company, and my customers. By discovering what made them tick, I could easily offer them the right product, or motivate and encourage people to bring in business. The ability to build rapport with others is something that some of us have naturally, but it can also be learned.

When promoted to my first branch manager position, I was told that the branch operates on its own and wouldn't grow or expand much. All I needed to do was just show up and maintain the status quo. I released this limiting belief and decided to make a difference and grow this branch, in spite of their low expectations. Besides, I liked a challenge! I networked with key people in the community and asked them for business referrals. I built a strong, motivated team by empowering them to think outside the box about ways to bring in business and made sure we provided excellent customer service at all times through staff training and recognition. We created "lunch and learns" at local businesses, built great relationships with lawyers, accountants, and real estate agents, and held periodic customer appreciation nights. It was essential for my staff and I to know who the important contacts were, and we were certain to show our appreciation to them. I also made it a point to always recognize my team for their dedication and hard work. After a couple of years, I was honoured as Manager of the Year, and the little branch I was given — the same one they said would never grow — exceeded everyone's expectations.

Value

WHAT A PERSON values is what creates their behaviour and what motivates them to do things. I have mentioned some of the items that motivated my mom and what she valued. How is it, then, that we can gain a better understanding of people? What a person values affects their choices in life, such as their jobs, friends, partners, hobbies, and purchases, where they live, or how they spend their time.

In NLP (neuro-linguistic programming) training, I learned a phrase that made a tremendous impact on me.

The phrase was, "Respect people's model of the world."

Each of us is different, and looking at things from someone else's perspective provides us with a clearer understanding of that individual. The more we understand about a person, the easier it is for us to communicate and connect with them.

How does a person decide what is of value to them? What they value is formed over certain periods of one's life, so it's not always a conscious or sudden decision. Our values are developed over long periods of time. Growing up, you learn from your parents, family members, and the world around you — your environment. You're told what's right and wrong, and all of this is instilled within you and becomes your set of values — your paradigm. As you mature, you become your own person and have your own opinions, and you judge others based on them. You may have role models who inspire you, teach you lessons, and help you create your beliefs and determine what is important to you. All that you learn and experience helps create what is important to you — your values.

So how can knowing all this help us when networking? What a person values helps us understand why a person does something, so if you are selling someone a service or managing employees, knowing what makes them decide or motivates them is essential. Many people assume things based on their own assumptions and what they value, not the individual they are dealing with. That is a mistake. We are all individuals, and what's important to one person may not be important at all to another. To find out a person's values is easy — all you need to do is ask the questions:

"What's important to you about ____?"

You can fill in the blank with whatever you are trying to offer them, like a new car, a house, taking a job, joining a group, or making any number of decisions. Their answers may be that they care about price, certain features, security, flexibility, and location. One person looking for a new home may be most concerned about the location (close to work), while another may be most interested in a big yard (for their children). Neither is wrong, but to understand their motivations (career versus family), you must identify what it is that matters most to them.

Once you fully understand what a person values, you'll be able to know what they want and speak to that desire. Now, a person may have an entire list of what's important to them, and they may rank some as more important than others. Ask for them to name their top three. When I receive a call about my services, I first find out about the individual — what they want, who they are, what's important to them — before I start telling them what I have to offer. So many people just go into their infomercial speech without knowing what the person's needs are; they often lose an opportunity. As a coach, I deal with many clients, helping them achieve their goals. Knowing what's important to them is the first thing we discuss, as some people aren't clear on this. They haven't given enough thought to their desires; they just "want." Once we define them, it is our guide to help get them to their (now well-defined and prioritized) goals. It provides them with a checkpoint to see if they have reached a goal.

It's All about Perception

EVERYONE HAS DIFFERENT items they value within themselves, such as security, physical fitness, respect, honesty, or making money. Values are different for everyone, and this knowledge opens your eyes, giving you a clearer understanding about yourself and others. When you network, you are building a bond. Knowing how others perceive communication helps to build the bond faster and make it stronger. I've learned great techniques to enhance my communications skills through my years in the corporate world, and my NLP training included how to read people by listening to their words and watching their body language.

How do we perceive information? Some of us are visual, so we need to see it. Some of us are kinesthetic, so we need to feel it. Some of us are auditory, so we need to hear it. And some people are auditory-digital, so they need lots of information, details, and facts. We can also be a combination of these things. Do you know what type of communicator you are?

Here's a sample chart to provide more information:

VISUAL	AUDITORY	KINESTHETIC	AUDITORY-DIGITAL
Need to see things or imagine how things look	Need to hear things and likes sounds	Need to feel and touch	Need to understand the details, get information, and make sense of it
HERE ARE SOME WORDS THEY MAY USE:			
Look See Show Picture this	Ring a bell Listen Hear Sounds like	Feel Hold Grasp Gut feeling	Sense Understand Think Perceive

ONCE YOU KNOW what style a person is, you can start using words and your body language to build instant rapport. When you know a person's communication style, you can start speaking their language. Below are some examples of sentences using each of the different types.

- **VISUAL:** When I **show** you how easy it is to attract clients to your business and you see how **good** it **looks**, you'll want to do it. You will see the benefits and how **attractive** it is.

- **AUDITORY:** This new product **sounds** great. You may have **heard** of it and the great benefits it offers. I can tell you all about it and the many features it has. If this **sounds** good, we can **discuss** it.

- **KINESTHETIC:** I will help you **grasp** this new idea on how to grow your business. Once you get a **hold** of new clients and get in **touch** with what's important to them, they'll buy. You'll know you are a success and will just **feel it in your gut.**

- **AUDITORY-DIGITAL:** I **sense** that you require more **details. I think** that once you go through all the **information,** it will make sense to you and you'll **understand.**

HAVE YOU EVER met someone and you just felt instantly connected and thought, *I really like that person.* You are in rapport with them. You can learn to intentionally create this same feeling with others. As mentioned above, you can use the words they are using (called mirroring) in your conversation with them. You know the visual person will need pictures or to be shown things so they appeal to them. The kinesthetic communicator you must let feel what they are looking at or use words to give them the perception of feeling it. The auditory people will need to hear things. The auditory-digital person needs lots of details and information, and it has to make sense to them.

Body Language

NOT ONLY DOES your language play a role in building rapport, so does your body.

How can body language play a role? By matching a person's body movement, it puts you in sync with them. They will feel connected to you. When I meet someone, I listen immediately to their words to find out their preferences as mentioned above and speak their language, but I'll also match their body movements. If they raise their hand to touch their face, I'll do the same, but in a restrained, unnoticeable way. If they cross their arms, I'll cross my arms, and if we are sitting and they cross their legs, I'll cross my legs. This works. Just be careful that it's not too obvious and overt, or it will look like you're mimicking them. It must be subtle; again, it's called mirroring.

The pace of their speaking plays a role too. I'll listen to how fast or slow they are speaking and try to match their speed. Have you ever talked to someone and maybe you speak quickly and they speak slowly, so having a conversation seems a little awkward? Pacing your voice is an easy and simple thing to do. So is matching their body movements. Try it out at your next meeting, whether it's a business meeting or a casual one with friends or family. How do you tell if you are in rapport with someone? It's easy. If you have successfully matched their words and body and you think you are in rapport, try changing your body and see if they follow. If you are in rapport with them, they will follow your body movement. If you uncross your legs or arms they may just uncross theirs. It's amazing to watch. You can also break rapport with this technique if you want to. Just start doing everything they aren't. If they talk slow, talk fast, or if they lean back, you lean forward into their space, purposely mismatching them. It's one way to get rid of someone — to get someone to leave your office for instance — which sometimes is a good thing!

I hope this information helps you with your business and improves your networking skills. Believe in yourself, understand others and what is important to them, and build rapport through your words and body language by observing and listening to figure out what type of person they are, and match it. Understanding people is easy if you just take the time and make the effort to focus, listen, watch, and follow suit. You just have to put your mind

some simple techniques, and, before you know it, you'll be
ationships with ease and your existing ones will be stronger.
mind does matter!

About Corey McCusker

COREY MCCUSKER is a life coach, motivational speaker, and author. She is certified as a master practitioner of neuro-linguistic programming (NLP), Time Empowerment Techniques™, and hypnosis. In 2006, she left the corporate world to follow her dreams and passions. She founded Your Mind Matters, a unique private coaching and training practice designed to help people take control of their lives by harnessing the power of their minds. Corey has assisted people in supercharging their lives, be it their health, wealth, career, relationships, or sports performance. In addition, Corey founded Muttz with Mannerz, a dog obedience school, which is another one of her passions. She practices what she preaches, is living the life she wants, and loves it!

Your Mind Matters
Relax + Release = Results!

Please visit Corey at
www.yourmindmatters.ca

Chapter VII

SPIRIT IS EVERYTHING

BY YVETTE MAXWELL

Chapter VII

SPIRIT IS EVERYTHING
by Yvette Maxwell

"Take the leap and build your wings on the way down."
— Paul Brandt

We all have those inspirational messages come across our desks every now and then, and some of them we hold on to and use as our mantras — words to live by. For me there have been a few good ones, but the one that has stood out the most is this: ***It is not a matter of whether you can or can't, it is whether you will or won't.***

This is so true. We all have the power to at least **try** — to "give it a go," if you will. It is not at all that we can't; it's rather that we don't or won't. Why is that? We can all find our own tailor-made excuses or reasons (those that make the most amount of sense to us personally) why we can't go for that other job, why we won't get up in front of a group of people and talk, why we won't forge ahead and pioneer a new standard in our line of business. The reasons could go on forever — we have given ourselves a choice — there is always a choice. The decision we make, the side we choose, we have to live with and face the consequences of that choice every day.

While in school, I realized my strongest desire was for helping people. I just didn't know exactly how. My marks were nowhere near good enough for medical school, so I explored my options. At that time, the alternative health care world was flourishing and there was just about a vitamin or mineral that could help any condition. Having worked in a pharmacy for years, natural medicine drew my interest. The interest veered off into the rehabilitation world and the various healing techniques.

I settled on massage therapy as my way of helping others heal. During school and into the initial years of opening my own practice, my passion for the work grew. In a time when this industry was engaged in a battle for

68

recognition as true health care providers, I was in the front lines of the fight, standing my ground with chiropractors and physiotherapists, questioning why we as massage therapists should, or could not be, included in the treatment of certain conditions. In the twelve years I've practiced massage therapy, this field has advanced by leaps and bounds, and I don't foresee it slowing at all. We have helped thousands and, as a result, have gained tremendous respect in the rehab community — and rightfully so.

Did my love of making people feel good have to be in the treatment room only? Was I limited to clients only? How could I reach more people? I have only two hands — that were, by the way, getting tired just with my existing client base. What next? I knew I didn't want a new profession, just to perhaps recreate my current one in some way. Could I do that? Did I even need someone to give me permission to do something else? To grow?

As I searched within my local massage therapy community, I realized there was too much rivalry among therapists to band together and learn each other's strengths and weaknesses to make sure that clients were getting the best care available to them. This was not even open to discussion. Having said that, however, I have formed some great relationships over the years with fellow therapists who are willing to refer clients to our clinic, and we reciprocate the same way when needed. I would much rather know that a client is going to a good clinic up the road, to someone who perhaps specializes in their particular needs, than just moving down to the next listing in the phone book. We learned about each other, our techniques, and our specialties, and we discovered more about each other's businesses. It was collaboration in the very best sense of the word, and we all felt we were giving our clients the best opportunity to heal and to feel better because of it.

The Next Step

NETWORKING WAS MY next step. I didn't have any other options. I needed to find out what everyone else was doing, so it was a natural step to join a group of professionals who openly discuss not only their jobs and their wares but also their dreams. Some self-employed clients told me about groups that they were a part of that they had found beneficial. I visited them all as a guest, and found varying degrees of discussions surrounding advertising, business presentations, and so forth. I did not find anything that made me feel comfortable. So the search continued. I was determined to find "something else," and to do "more."

My next realization was that just like my dream had to work for me, so did the networking. I needed to feel welcome, valuable, and respected. An absolute requirement was to be surrounded by those who were in the same boat. Yes, I wanted to hear the most common mistakes people make with respect to advertising. It was important to know someone could help with my bookkeeping, decorate for Christmas, teach me how to make baby food, and even sell me my funeral plot for when this ride was over. But were they feeling the same emotions as me from a personal perspective?

Growing a business is difficult and requires all of your efforts, but you still need to have contact with the outside world, to know that there are others trying to do the same as you, fighting the same battle. I needed to know that there were other souls out there lying awake in bed at night like me, mulling over last month's statements, wondering if I could do this with young children, deciding which tradeshow to be a part of; that someone else has nothing to wear to that important meeting, or that someone else is in major overdraft with the bank. "Please, God, let me know that I am not the only one," I prayed. What comfort I found with a great networking group. Intelligent conversations based on business growth, inspiring individuals all trying to make a concrete contribution to their world, and, in the midst of it all, great laughter.

For me, everything always has to happen at the same time; my life is chaotic. I need my "calm life" in the treatment room, with the sound effects of birds singing and waves crashing on some faraway seashore. There is always pure chaos everywhere else. Those who know me well have a tremendously hard time understanding how I can go into a treatment room, give someone a therapeutic massage for an hour, induce relaxation with the music, the candles, the dim lighting, and speaking softly. They don't see how it is possible for me to do that, because it's not — or doesn't appear to be — in my nature. I am the outgoing, loud one causing trouble in the back of the room. But that is my business, and I do it well. You do what you have to do to make it happen when it's your livelihood. And I do enjoy it tremendously, which is, after all, the best part. Do what you have to do, and give yourself no choice — no other option but to do what's necessary.

My long-time best friend and personal business consultant taught me that, together with "Always aim for perfection — always," which has become another mantra. She has been a main part of my success and support group. And now that she has unfortunately moved across the country, we share many a cup of tea during long chats over the phone. Even in all the chaos of business growth and expansion, she is one of my steady rocks. We all need those kinds of loyal people in our lives to help us be successful. I am lucky to have a few, and one of them is my wonderful husband. Remember, everything always happens at the same time.

If it Is to Be, Then it Is Up to Me

WHEN I DECIDED to start Hands in Demand, I thought the timing was perfect. I had worked in the community for a few years and built up a steady, loyal client base. I was newly married and saving money for a house. No time like the present, right? "Let's do it, jump in with both feet," I declared. I had the support and blessings of family and friends, and the bank, though not the most important, perhaps, was a big factor. Great! I found space that could be transformed into what I needed, so I signed a five-year lease. I was raring to go, ready to treat till my hands fell off so I could pay the loan back as quickly as possible. After all, I was young, eager, strong, and (did I mention?) pregnant.

So, remember that sage advice — don't give yourself a choice? Now the words of wisdom that once made so much sense were going to get pitched out the window. Are you kidding me? How was I going to treat all day feeling like I was going to heave all over the client? Where was all my energy? It had vanished overnight. How was I going to do this? "This was not the plan!" I screamed. The dream was changing (again). And I had no choice but to change with it. **To evolve.** I quickly decided that there was no way I was going to be able to show up for work each day if I did not get enough rest or proper food. So I came in rested, brought my wheelbarrow-sized lunch, and even napped between bookings. It helped that my parents owned a restaurant nearby, so quick snacks and even delivery could always be arranged. In fact, I learned that my support system was readily available — who wants to mess with a pregnant, broke entrepreneur? Sometimes you don't know your support system is in place until you need to lean on them.

Without a doubt, by the time my first son was a year old, I felt like those first eighteen months of the business had gone by like a whirlwind. It was a period that I would not have survived without the support of my husband and family. My mother knew all the answers as to why the baby would not stop crying, and my husband knew enough to keep the house clean and to support me no matter what. The support for me was essential. I am strong-willed enough to do it on my own, no doubt, but when you have those around you who can make the road easier, be grateful and take it! Take the help; don't deny others the opportunity to feel good about helping you.

One of the other main lessons I learned was that it is okay to admit you need help, and it is okay to ask for it. Part of that whole superwoman persona — "Not to worry. I can do it," "Yes, of course I have time to do that" — never mind that rubbish. That was one of the hardest lessons for me to learn. Asking for help is part one of that lesson; part two is learning to say no. Surprisingly, once you start saying no, it becomes easier, and then you find yourself saying no much more often. Telemarketers, PTA groups, family invites, and even staff sometimes get a simple no from me. Saying no feels great, once you get used to it. Very empowering. You have created your surroundings — take responsibility for them.

But What about Me?

SO, ALL WAS well. Business was steadily growing. I survived maternity leave (all six weeks) with no income (ah, one of the hidden beauties of self-employment), and I was raring to go. Now, mind you, I couldn't work more hours; I had a dependant child at home. My support system was unwavering, as was my passion for my work. So the everyday race began. I had to take care of the baby, take care of the business, take care of staff, and take care of the house, and on and on it went. I had help, and lots of it, but there still never seemed to be enough hours in the day. I'm not sure where I would be today without it. Some days my husband and mother saw each other more than they saw me, but it had to be done. Right?

Hard work will be rewarded, I've always believed. My eastern European background, combined with the fact that my parents owned a restaurant, taught me that there is no such thing as rest until the work is done. My parents also taught me that a strong work ethic will get you far in life, and I believed them. My business and I are proof of it; however, I've tweaked it just a bit. There has to be a limit. What I was forgetting in all this chaos and madness was that I had forgotten about me. I have a passion for helping people feel better. Everyone deserves to feel that state of relaxation one gets after a great massage therapy treatment. Everyone should take time for themselves (including me). When was the last time, I wondered one day, I had done that for myself?

Exhaustion, physical aches and pains, and mental and emotional stress aren't good for business. Not to mention home life. I certainly didn't want to tick off those who were trying their best to keep me sane. But I did need to take care of myself. Feeling stressed, rushed, and pressured does not bode well for calculated business decisions. And who wants to visit a massage therapist who looks like she's been run over by a truck? In order to foster growth and evolution, you need to be able to think clearly. Being able to look at life and business from a calm, honest, educated, and professional perspective allows you to make progressive decisions that increase your bottom line. This is not to say at all that there will not be times of pressure or stress where quick, last-minute decisions or ranking priorities will have to be made. It is simply to say that taking care of yourself first and getting to a place where you are able to take time for yourself each and every day will, without a doubt, directly impact your business, your health, and your life. The question is, How are you going to do that? When? How long? Don't wait — start now. Make a plan, and, when possible, stick to it.

Look at your situation, and find what works for you. Sort it out. My world really went upside down when my second son was born. It spun even more when he was eighteen months old and I decided to expand the clinic and take over new space. This meant leasehold improvements, so back to the bank it was. If you ever need to blow off steam, put some contractors in your life and tell them what you really think — it was seriously some of the best fun I have ever had. I managed the supermom act a bit better the second time around. (Although, I do want to track that woman down who told me that the second child would be a breeze.) He has many of my traits, and, thus, I have met my match.

Take my advice: Learn to love your designated "me time," whether it is simply taking a bath, walking the dog, or drinking a quiet cup of tea. Whatever it was that I could squeeze in, I needed a little bit of time to myself, and so do you. To this day, my most favourite activity is to wake up very early in the morning, before everyone else, and share quiet time with just myself and my thoughts. Honestly, it keeps me sane. We teach our kids to do this all the time and forget to do it in our adult lives. Why is this? Now, I'm not referring to a vacation. That has an entirely different purpose. The time I'm talking about is for reflection, for strategizing, for pondering and gratitude, and, most of all, for just "being" — every day. It is all right to just "be still." You're not being lazy or unproductive, and there are probably a hundred things you could be doing, but none of them are as important as your personal, private "me time." I've taught clients this for years, and some were far ahead of me in the "me" department. It is okay to take time for yourself. Listen to some quiet music, dance to some loud music, take a walk, reread your favourite book, or watch an inspiring movie. Make a wish list, or just dream. It is okay to just be."

Currently, I'm surrounded by a group of fabulous ladies who have all made a choice. They continue to make choices — ones that hopefully bring them closer to their dreams. Live your dream, and achieve happiness, right? Yes, but that dream has to be created, nourished, and grown. For some, the dream is simple: Leave my corporate job and work out of my basement selling a fabulous product that I have created. For others, the dream is much more complex and involved. One major lesson that networking has taught me (and there are many) is that there are very different versions of "the dream" out there. We each have our own, after all, and truth be told, if we have nothing to work towards, then why are we here, right? We all need purpose, and we all need to feel as if our life matters. If you don't have a dream, large or small, then why have you picked up this book? The point is that it doesn't matter what the dream is, as long as you have one. Our dreams push and pull us through life, exerting tremendous pressure and forcing us to answer the hard questions. The true exercise lies in whether or not your dream is going to be the same next year. I would like to tell you that not only is it is okay if it is not, but, in fact, I also believe that it is far better if it is tweaked somewhat when necessary. In other words, it's a dream, not a stone tablet. The evolution of our lives brings about change, which brings about growth. Evolution is a good thing.

So, as Hands in Demand has evolved, so have I. We all evolve as people, and recognizing our changing circumstances is healthy. We change our tastes (who likes the same foods or the same styles they did when they were in high school?), our surroundings (we move, change jobs), and our passions (our lovers, mates, and life passions). For entrepreneurs, we create our lives based on those very things. If they change, so does the business. Increased business often comes with change and adaptation. Where is your business headed? Are you keeping up? Take care of yourself first, stay in touch with your passion, and you will be able to keep up. Stay strong, and have courage. All those roads lead to success.

Take time for yourself, and feel better. Your spirit will grow and shine.

About Yvette Maxwell

YVETTE MAXWELL is a Registered Massage Therapist specializing in chronic pain, overuse injuries, and stress management. Her BA with honours in medical anthropology nicely complements her well-rounded and informed approach to health care and rehabilitation.

Hands in Demand Therapeutic Massage Company was founded on the principle of bringing quality therapeutic massage treatments into the community as well as increasing public knowledge on the wide scope of conditions that massage therapy can benefit.

Through her own hectic family schedule as well as clinic ownership and previous massage therapy faculty membership, she has learned the lesson first-hand that stress in our lives is optional, but learning how to deal with it is not. She enjoys teaching techniques that allow us to take a step back, relax, and get ready to confront stress.

"Take time for yourself, and FEEL BETTER."

Please visit Yvette at
www.handsindemand.ca

Chapter VIII

THE PIXIE DUST FACTOR

BY CARLA SEGATO

Chapter VIII

THE PIXIE DUST FACTOR
by Carla Segato

It is all about the pixie dust. Armed with only a sprinkling of pixie dust and the touch of a magic wand, how did a pint-sized fairy with a blonde "updo," a green, shaggy dress, and a sassy attitude transform the world? Let me take you on a journey through my very own Never Land. Come along, and you'll learn that Tinker Bell doesn't just live in the Disney theme parks or in Pixie Hollow, the land of fairies. She actually lives within each of us. You will discover there is pixie dust inside of you just waiting to be sprinkled. You'll also discover that everything you are looking for is out there looking for you. I'll show you how giving a little magic goes a long way to getting you exactly what you want. Best of all, you'll help the people around you achieve their goals and dreams as you bridge the gap between where you are and where you want to be.

How Dreams Really Do Come True

WE ALL HAVE special gifts and talents. Our job is to discover and share them with the world. I have learned that the more you give away, the more there is that comes back to you. Not necessarily from the direct source you are dealing with, but from "The Source." The world operates according to universal laws. It is like gravity — even if you don't believe, it still exists and is still at work. The absence of evidence is not the evidence of absence. The premise of the universal laws is that on a microscopic, cellular level, we are energy: a mass of electrons and atoms that spin rapidly. Energy moves in a circular fashion. Our thoughts, feelings, words, and actions all form an energy circle and come back to us, so it is important to choose them carefully. Quite simply, what we focus our attention on is then manifested or created in a physical form. It's exactly why I am writing this chapter, and exactly why you are reading it.

The Wonderful World of Disney

LIKE MOST KIDS, I was crazy about Mickey and Minnie Mouse, Donald, Pluto, and Goofy, referred to within The Walt Disney Corporation as the Fab Five. Every Sunday, without fail, I would sit on the sofa and watch The Wonderful World of Disney on television. I was especially drawn to Tinker Bell, because she was the magic-maker. I wanted to be one too — to be a maker of magic. That was my fantasy.

Many years later, my fantasy was about to become my reality. Disney was looking for someone to manage their marketing, events, and promotions. My boss recommended me for the job. I was excited and frightened all at the same time — after all, I was going to the place where real magic was made! The pixie dust was stirring. I travelled to Orlando to experience the Spanish Inquisition version of interviewing with all the Disney executives. I was hired and received my mouse ears and a silver pin, which read "Dream" — the basis of Walt Disney's philosophy.

I went to Walt Disney World to learn the secrets of the Disney magic and the Disney traditions, better known as the policies and procedures. My job as an international senior marketing executive was to promote the Disney theme parks that are in Florida, California, and Paris. I filled my briefcase with pixie dust, and began one of the most rewarding and interesting periods in my life, during which I needed lots of networking magic.

Networking is critical to your success — and it is not just away from work, it is inside your work as well. It is those employee relationships and partnerships that make the magic happen. And it did.

Networking in large corporations with global properties and interests and attempting to find your way around is like trying to crack the Da Vinci code, or sorting out a big dysfunctional family. You need to get to know everyone and their roles in the "big family." Not only do you have to learn the house rules, you also need to learn the unique language spoken there. Disney has a language too. It is based on theatrical terminology. The parks and resorts are the stages where everything is themed to the smallest detail and played out daily before millions. The employees are called "cast members" because they are playing a role in the theme park experience. They are taught to conduct themselves as if they are always on stage. The visitors are "guests" because they experience the production.

Working for The Walt Disney Corporation was such an impressionable experience, I felt like a branded calf. Once you see how the masters work, the Disney rules of customer service and high standards become imprinted in your DNA. These Disney success codes and the pixie dust philosophy became integrated in all I did. In fact, former colleagues and clients still call me Tink.

Disney employees are trained to create that magic wherever they are and with whomever they meet. It was called "pixie dusting," or "aggressively servicing," which means looking for ways to enhance someone's experience, not merely waiting for a guest to ask for something. These small gestures translate into the overarching message: You are important.

Another opportunity to show people they are important is when things go wrong. And no matter how hard everyone works, mistakes will happen and things will go awry. It happens in business (and in life) every day. That's when the pixie dust really flies. My Disney customer service training taught me not to just make it right, but to make it right and memorable! Without exception, correct the problem immediately and then give a little extra. This is also what we call "pixie dusting." It applies to everything we do. Anyone can produce what is expected of them, but not everyone will go the extra distance. Companies know that customer experiences create lasting impressions and that *word-of-mouth* advertising or network marketing is how they get their greatest repeat business. Or not.

Let me give an example. Let's say that guests — a family of four — arrive at their Disney hotel and their room is not ready for them to be able to check in. In addition to apologizing the Disney cast member informs the guest of the exact time they can expect their room to be ready. The guest's luggage is safely stored and they are given a coupon for a free meal to enjoy while they wait on their room.

When those guests return home, they are going to tell people that they had "the most fabulous meal at the Contemporary Resort" and that it was "absolutely free of charge." A potentially bad experience was magically transformed into a memorable one with a little pixie dust.

Listen for the i

FOR THE CORPORATE structu
by the rules and learn the dance, or, as I u.
Unfortunately some companies demand so much n.
leaves them depleted, exhausted, and unhappy because they a.
time with the people who really matter. If you have found yourseh ..
where you are not flourishing, chances are the work environment is siphoning
off your energy. Most people start to panic and do things to fit in. For some
strange reason, we are willing to forgo our innate desire to stretch and grow,
and we would rather stay in a place that takes our energy instead of giving us
energy.

We are sometimes afraid to leave this environment, because we believe
it supports us and defines us, and, without the strong arms of the company
pension plan, we are without security. I have experienced first-hand that this
is not the truth. If you have witnessed today's current events in the banking
and stock markets, then you know that security is elusive. Security is just a
feeling inside that you interpret from your circumstances. Security is not a
job or bank account tally, both of which can be gone tomorrow. Security
must come from within.

There came a point in my career when I had a great entrepreneurial
desire to create a job or business that would give me freedom and more time
to do with it as I chose. I, too, was still battling my old fear paradigms of
leaving my well-paid management job to risk it all and go it on my own. But
the real risk was not to have tried and to let the energy of heartfelt desires go
unfulfilled.

After reading *Think and Grow Rich* by Napoleon Hill, I came to
understand that all successful people, without exception, did the same two
things to achieve their dreams: They wrote their goals on a card and carried
it with them at all times, and they practiced daily visualization. Following in
Hill's footsteps, I created my own card and wrote down my dream job wish
list. I wasn't sure if such a job even existed, because there was no job title on
any Internet job sites that matched my criteria!

y list read as follows: Be my own boss; time and freedom to walk g on the beach and practice yoga every morning; travel the world; a six- or seven-figure salary; have fun; work with like-minded, positive dividuals; feel appreciated and valued; and make a big difference in people's ves. What was it going to be? What could it be? I knew it was not going to be working as a missionary or corporate warrior, but beyond that, my magical career was without definition.

Opportunity knocks many times in our lives, but it often passes us by because we are so focused on what we think it *should* look like that we end up missing it completely. My opportunity came cloaked in a form that I was certain was a huge mistake. It was marketing a product through a distribution model called "network marketing." I'm not sure what it was about the term "network marketing" that made me want to run and hide, but it did. I had to actually stop and examine my severe reaction.

What did I really know about network marketing? I'd never had any experience doing it, so I couldn't say I'd had a poor one. I realized that my belief system about network distribution was inherited or adopted from other people. It was *not* based on fact or first-hand experience at all. I remember my friend and mentor, Bob Proctor of the hit movie *The Secret,* saying, "Carla, don't ask your neighbours what they think you should do. If you asked most people what they were thinking, they would be speechless. Most people confuse mental activity with thinking." Bob was right.

I believe that people, things, circumstances, and opportunities come into your life for a reason. Too often, we overthink matters instead of listening to the quiet voices inside of us, which are called our "gut" feelings. GUT is just an acronym for global universal truth. I recalled this famous quote from Napolean Hill's, *Think & Grow Rich:* "Notable individuals have the courage to pursue their dreams and not be persuaded by public opinion."

It was at that moment I started to do my research on the network marketing industry. I realized that, like me, most people had an antiquated opinion of the industry and were not up to date on the growth and changes that had taken place. This was now a business of professionals and executives as well as stay-at-home parents who were part of the "new economy," where top-notch products are sold through relationship or referral marketing. It is the last affordable model of free enterprise that exists.

In 2007 in the United States, fifteen million people were network marketing distributors with over $30 billion in sales. I figured out it would be somewhat difficult to fool fifteen million people. I clarified that a pyramid scheme was not network marketing. Pyramid schemes are illegal, but network marketing companies are governed by strict regulations. People share and recommend movies, restaurants, and products all the time. In network marketing, the companies pay you for the recommendation. It was a terrific and rewarding experience for me. In my presentations, I would often say that I spent years climbing the corporate ladder to find out it was up against the wrong wall, and it was true.

This opportunity came to me because it was a direct match to the goals I had set for myself, and the perfect way of making a living. It was a life worth living. It was a law of attraction match. When my husband and I moved to Hong Kong, we continued to build our network marketing business. Living in Asia I came to understand the deep cultural importance and honor of giving a personal referral or recommendation and that's why countries such as China, Korea, Taiwan and Japan are giants in the network marketing profession. Unlike North America, it is as noble a profession as a doctor or lawyer. My passion for the industry and for helping people achieve their dreams paved the way for my future work. As a senior management executive, I consulted network marketing companies in the United States in the area of event planning and marketing. I have since trained thousands of distributors, encouraging them to take the road less travelled and to follow their passions, not their paycheques.

Walter Elias Disney was a man of great vision and big dreams. Before his big dream became a reality, he networked with many people to look for investors. He shared the opportunity with his friend, Art Linkletter, who relates a wonderful story about the time that Walt took him out to the future site of Disneyland, which was in the middle of the orange groves of Anaheim, California. Walt described his dream of building this magical theme park to which people would come from all over the world. It would be for children and adults to enjoy. It would be called Disneyland — the happiest place on Earth. He did not believe in Walt's vision and declined the invitation to join in a joint venture with him. Mr. Linkletter continues the story by saying, "Walt and I walked back to our cars, and it was a long walk. I have since figured out that by not seeing Walt's vision and joining his venture, each step I took back to the car cost me about one million dollars!"

:s in life, you have to believe it **before** you see it, not the
id. Everyone could use a little pixie dust magic. If you look
ju might just discover that you are the one holding the magic

About
Carla
Segato

CARLA SEGATO is an international marketing, communications, and event-planning specialist and a management consultant. Carla has lived and worked globally, including taking assignments in Hong Kong, Dallas, Texas, Los Angeles, and Toronto. Ms. Segato was recruited for her expertise by the international division of The Walt Disney Corporation, was the former director of marketing and communications for CFRB Newstalk Radio, and has worked extensively in the United States in executive management for a number of highly successful network marketing companies.

Carla has a passion for inspiring people to reach their lifelong dreams. She has mentored and trained, and changed the lives of thousands of professionals worldwide.

Please visit Carla at
www.pixiedustcommunications.com

Chapter IX

CAPITALIZE YOUR VALUE

BY JOANNE FERNS

Chapter IX

CAPITALIZE YOUR VALUE
by Joanne Ferns

I'm not sure if it is my professional designation as a Certified General Accountant (CGA), my twenty plus years' experience servicing business owners and entrepreneurial organizations, or a combination of both that leads me to translate everything back to the mighty dollar. I am certain that over the years I've discovered that while the symbols may vary from country to county, the currency sign still remains the universal language of business.

I've also come to agree with this, and not just for business but for everything we do. You may be thinking I must have a very materialistic approach to life. In fact, it is just the opposite. You see, you may see the dollar symbol as money, and that would be a fair conclusion if this were the case. But, for me, I see this symbol as a representation of much more, and perhaps that is where we differ. To me, the dollar symbol represents not just money, but value. To truly make the most of and get the most out of life, as individuals, we must create exceptional value in all that we do, both personally and professionally.

Pretend for a moment that I just gave you a million dollars and said, "Do with it what you will." What would you do? I bet you're already thinking of an exciting vacation (Australia, Baja…those are on my top ten list), visualizing your new car (metallic silver Porsche for me), or, perhaps, thinking of gifts you will buy for family and friends. See? It took nothing for us to decide how to spend that money. So why is it we cannot all put the same decisiveness and determination into our lives? After all, we are spending them — the days of our lives — carelessly and frivolously or wisely, just like money. There may be such a thing as life everlasting, but our time here on Earth is not infinite. So how do you wish to be remembered? What do you have that you can leave for others to remember and enjoy? And, even more important, what can you do with this while you are here on Earth? You can make a difference, but first you must determine your *value.*

Exploration

THE FIRST PART of our journey is the exploration to discover our inherent value. Every great feat in life was started with the quest of discovery. Christopher Columbus sailed to the Americas; Neil Armstrong was the first to set foot on the moon. These discoveries looked outward, but they began within. They had a strong sense of purpose and passion to be persistent until they accomplished what they set out to achieve. Our exploration will focus on the power within that leads us to great outward achievements!

Like any great journeyer, you'll need to prepare. There is only one rule for this journey, and you need to agree upon it before we start. The rule is this: You are 100 percent responsible for you. If you will not take responsibility for yourself, then you can't possibly tap into your full potential, as you are undoubtedly enabling those around you to map out your journey. That is not to say we can't allow others to share our journey and play important roles within it. That is what shapes us. My point is simply this: We cannot blame others for what we have failed to do. To get started on this journey, you will need to pack a few items to take with us. The first critical item is one you always have with you — the six inches between your ears, a.k.a. "The Mind." This has the power to help or hinder, so we need to use it wisely. You will also need to pack a timer or stopwatch to keep you focused and on track, and paper and a pen for writing down discovery revelations. Last, but certainly not least, you should find a "discovery" place that is very relaxing and thought-provoking for you. Somewhere without external distractions, and where you find peace and can get in touch with your inner self.

Once you have all these elements in place, you are ready to take the journey toward your future. On a piece of paper, in large letters across the top, write down ***"Things I Do Well."*** We are going to make a list. In just a moment, I will ask you to set the timer for seven minutes. This will allow you to focus on getting in touch with the "true you" and not worry about anything around you. You have dedicated your next seven minutes to our journey of discovery, and only after the timer goes off can you allow the outside world to form part of our journey again. Before you press start, I am going to provide the rest of the instructions. After all, none of us have the unique talent of seeing with our eyes closed!

1. Close your eyes and find your own unique calming, peaceful "mind" place. You may travel around the world, or find yourself sitting on a rock by the ocean listening to the waves splash all around you. Or it may be easier for you to look for a white light and focus on looking into that light. Whatever works for you.

2. You will now take ten deep breaths. Breathe in slowly to the count of three, and focus on what is happening to your body — chest expanding; abdomen contracting — now, slowly exhale to the count of five…everything is relaxing. Feel yourself relax with each breath, and follow that breath as it moves throughout your body. With each breath, you move deeper and deeper into your soul. This is what you are searching for. The true meaning of life lies within, so let's not cut this trip short. After you complete your full count of ten, continue to sit for a moment in silence with your eyes still closed.

3. Ask yourself, "What am I really good at? When do I feel proud?" Think of this for a few seconds, and then open your eyes.

4. Now set your timer for seven minutes, pick up your pen, and start writing what comes to mind, under the heading **"Things I Do Well."**
   There are no prizes awarded for finishing first, or for having the most items on the list. You are really focusing on being in touch with the "true you." You see, each of us is unique in our own right. This is how we tap into our DNA (darn natural ability)!
   When the timer goes off, you should stop immediately. Did you stop? Be honest!

5. Reset the timer for five minutes.

6. Write down the following heading: **"What Do Others SAY I Do Well?"**

7. Write down everything that comes to mind. What do others (family, friends, and co-workers) compliment you on? Think hard about this and recall awards, conversations, and gratitude expressed by others. Have you noticed a common theme emerging?

LET ME SHARE this with you; maybe it will ring true for you, as well. For more than half my life, people often told me I would make a very good teacher. In my business career, I was commended often on my public speaking and presentation skills. I was also called upon when there was a problem. It seemed I was always the "go to" person for problem solving. Was this due to my fortuitous problem-solving skills or as a result of me regularly portraying my core beliefs: honesty, fairness, and integrity? This allowed me to always try to be objective and assess any problematic situation from both sides to find solutions that provide the greatest value.

You see, I have come to understand *(and it's taken a forty-year journey to get here)* that there's not much value in taking a trip to the Bahamas to lay on the beach with someone who thinks they are going to Iceland. Every relationship and every journey in life must hold a common ground. It is interesting how, upon reflection, we utilize these inner core values in all that we do, and, if allowed *(it is us that decides that, by the way)*, they can serve us well! How are you doing with this one? Keep going. If you are struggling, then I urge you to seek others' opinions. Don't be shy; ask and you shall receive, as our Heavenly Father has taught us.

For now, put down what you believe to be what others perceive, as the timer will go off shortly. Later, you can ask others and add to your list. So you now have two lists: one based on what you believe, and the other based on what others perceive you to be. Interesting, note whether or not there are any similarities in the two lists?

You are now starting to uncover your DNA, your unique talents that make you **YOU!** These talents create your **value.** How can this fulfill your **purpose** in life?

Let's dig a little deeper for a moment. Yes, more breathing and more paper. This time, I will ask you to take only a few moments (set the timer for two minutes, if you wish). Ask yourself, "What makes me me?" Write down the answer. "What are my core values and beliefs?" These are the feelings or emotional needs within us that need to be fulfilled. In my case above, I mentioned a few of mine: honesty and integrity, fairness to all concerned. Others might include health, family, a sense of accomplishment, wealth, or spirituality. Money is not on the list, as you can see. This is not because I do not see any value in it. My husband will tell you that I like to shop with the best of them. However, it is a tool — a means to an end. It is not and should not be a "value" in and of itself.

Money is certainly not part of my core values or beliefs. It is the pleasure I attain from activities involving the use of money. I also receive immense pleasure from saving money when I go shopping. There is nothing like the elation I feel when I can spend two hundred dollars on clothes that would have normally cost four hundred dollars if regularly priced. I saved my hard-working husband two hundred dollars! What a thoughtful wife I am. And I come home elated — on top of the world! There is much pleasure in this, trust me. It is not the money, it is the pleasure and feelings it provides me. Now every time I wear those bargain-priced clothes, I associate them with that feeling. The person who invented the word "sale" certainly knew the purpose they were fulfilling.

So, let's see what we have uncovered so far on our exploration together:

We have found you have some unique talents, and some deep core values that comprise who you are and what you feel strongly about. Herein lays the answer to the discovery of your purpose and passion in life. We all have them. A special gift bestowed upon us. This is the fire in your belly — it is what you believe in like no one else. You have **passion** for this. If you can ignite that **passion,** then you're on *fire*. You stand head and shoulders above the rest.

You see, people don't buy *things;* they buy what they believe those things *stand for.* It's true. Think of something you purchased lately. What was it? Why did you buy it? What need was it fulfilling? Loyalty? Recognition (brands do this well)? Prestige (status symbol labels)? Health? I don't drink milk to help feed the farmers; I drink it because I have been raised to believe it is good for our health: Calcium builds strong bones, and strong bones are healthy. Not everyone may agree with this, and that's all right. Our beliefs are personal, and that is why knowing and understanding your target audience is so important. We could go on and on, but the point is simple. Whatever we purchased, we did so to fulfill a need, and the one we purchased it from had the ability to reach out to us and make us feel their product/brand/service was going to meet the need best amongst the rest.

So now let me share with you my formula for capitalization of **value:**

Passion + Purpose = Prosperity

YOU MUST HAVE passion for what you do; this is what ignites you and allows you to express and share what you so uniquely have (this often sets you apart from all others). The purpose must be there too; this is the DNA, your unique talents and strengths that must be matched to those who need those talents or strengths.

Now, you may be thinking, *"That's great, but how do I get my message out?"* How do you discover if there is a need for your unique talent? While there are many ways to accomplish this, I recommend your very first step is to tap into what you already have and know.

Everyone has a personal network. The best part of tapping into your personal network (family, friends, associates, social acquaintances) is that they already know and love you. That's right: Your personal network is your deepest form of relationship. People don't belong to your personal network because they have to; it's because they want to. That's huge! They know you, they trust you, they love you, and they want what's best for you. Wow! I can't think of anyone else I would rather have to promote me and what I do than my mom, my family, my friends, and my colleagues. Before they can do this, you must reach out and ASK for their help. I hear people say time and time again that "They never help me," or "That's too much to ask." My response is simply a question back: "Have you ever asked them?" The resounding answer is nearly always, "NO!"

Think about this for a moment: They know you, they trust you, and they love you. You need only share with them what you do (your talents) and allow them to feel your passion (why you are so dedicated to this). Now they know what you stand for and why. And then you ask them to let others know about what you do. What do you think that will look like? They will reach out to others and carry your message for you! And herein lies what I call the **Exponential Factor.** That's marketing through the power of connecting. In modern times, also most commonly known as **networking!**

Passion and purpose may not be the sole secrets to success, but what I know for sure is that every successful person has those two common elements — passion and purpose — in their souls!

About

Joanne

Ferns

JOANNE FERNS is a certified coach, professional trainer, facilitator, and speaker. She has extensive knowledge in all facets of business — sales, marketing, operations, systems, employee relations, and finance — with over twenty years' experience working with business owners and senior executive teams to build business strategies for supporting sustained organizational growth. As a Certified General Accountant, she incorporates her solid background in strategic planning, finance, business valuations, and taxation into successful strategies. Honesty and integrity are of the utmost importance in everything Joanne does. As an independent owner of The Growth Coach, she is able to fulfill her passion and purpose, helping other entrepreneurs, professionals, and managers to make more money with less effort and to capitalize the value of their businesses and lives!

The Growth Coach is a leader in business coaching and optimization strategies to build valuable business organizations. The company provides one-on-one and group coaching, strategic retreats, and special project assistance to business owners, self-employed professionals, and managers. Through a **guaranteed** proven process, The Growth Coach has been helping business owners earn more and work less for over a decade.

Please visit Joanne at
www.thegrowthcoach.com/jferns

Chapter X

I'VE ALWAYS HAD A LOT OF CONFIDENCE — NOT!

BY ROSE-ANNE KUMPUNEN

Chapter X

I'VE ALWAYS HAD A LOT OF CONFIDENCE — NOT!

by Rose-Anne Kumpunen

"If you're not uncomfortable, then you're not growing. Push yourself to be the best you can be by taking risks and having the confidence and courage to put a voice to your passions."
— Rose-Anne

There I was, standing backstage peeking out from behind the curtain preparing to walk out, my hands sweating, my heart beating fast, yet everything appears to be happening in slow motion and spinning at the same time. Never mind...it's time. That's my cue. Out, I go to give the performance of my life to a full house. The lights shine in my eyes, I open my mouth, and — my mind goes blank! Why am I on stage again? I suddenly can't remember a single line. Finally, in desperation, I glance down and see my teacher/director start to sing my lines and wave her hands to conduct the choir. She smiles as she encourages me to sing along. Somehow I manage to snap back into my starring role as the Virgin Mary and quietly finish my solo with a heavy heart and cheeks so red and hot from humiliation that I could've fried a couple of eggs on them.

After that pivotal event in my life, most people would have understood if I chose to stay out of the spotlight forever. I'm sure many others suffering similar embarrassment have done just that. It was a life-changing moment for me for sure, and I was only ten years old. The next year, I shocked some of my friends, parents, and teachers, and even myself, when I auditioned for another solo. You see, for some reason, even though I was very young, I understood that I had to keep going for it, if performing solos was what I truly wanted to do. No matter how uncomfortable I might have felt inside.

Perhaps that's what started the illusion that I had a l
Years later, I found it strange when other people commented (
And I guess, looking back on the many times that I push
went after what I wanted, I did indeed have confidence. The interesting
aspect of this thought is that I didn't know it. I didn't feel confident; I felt
determined.

Finding Role Models to Inspire Confidence

IN MY LIFE, I was fortunate to have some great confident people
who helped me to believe that I was able to do whatever I wanted. They were
my role models, and they inspired confidence in me even when I didn't believe
that I could shape my life into anything I wanted. I utilized role models
repeatedly in both my personal and professional life. As a newbie entrepreneur
in my early twenties, I didn't know all that was involved in owning my own
business, so I looked to other people who were successful. What were they
doing that I liked? Where did they go to promote their businesses? How did
they talk about their companies?

Once I learned their techniques, I copied them. I thought if it
worked for them, it could work for me. For the most part, it did. One of the
primary challenges I faced with this was trying to stay the same "me" while
incorporating their business methods.

The Little-Known Secret to Confidence

*"The thing that is really hard, and really amazing, is giving up on being perfect
and beginning the work of becoming yourself."*
— Anna Quindlen

SOMETHING MUST HAVE happened to me on the way to starting
my business that made me believe I needed to do everything perfectly. And
I'm sure if we delved deep into the mind's eye of my childhood, there was
some event that burned this limiting belief into my subconscious. Because
that is what perfectionism is: a limiting belief. And it probably wouldn't be
the only one we'd discover. And if you took the time to look deeper into your

heart and your mind, you'd more than likely find a few of your own. Each one of us has a little voice in our head that whispers unkind words on occasion. "Stop." "You can't do that." "You're going to embarrass yourself." "That's not possible." "Who do you think you are to try that?" It's that internal dialogue we sometimes hear that we feel we don't have any control over. Hey, that's okay; we all have those conversations with ourselves. The key is to learn how to replace those negative words and limiting beliefs with positive ones with limitless possibilities.

So I'm going to share a secret with you. This one "secret" alone can truly make the difference between your being successful in your own business and continuing to struggle to make ends meet. Are you ready? Okay, ask yourself this question: What do all entrepreneurs need to succeed? The answer is simple: Confidence. So read this statement aloud and often: All entrepreneurs need to succeed is *confidence.*

What is confidence? If you look the term up in the dictionary, you'll find the definition as "freedom from doubt; belief in yourself and your abilities." Now, read that again — belief in yourself and your abilities. So, what do we all have to work through to acquire confidence? Our limiting beliefs. That little voice inside that tells us we're not good enough or smart enough or fast enough or clever enough.

Our beliefs are at the core of our being. They guide our decisions and behaviour in all areas of life — even our business decisions — and they determine what we think is or is not possible. Do we have to let our limiting beliefs control us? No! Can we actively make changes about our beliefs? Absolutely, yes! Take me, for instance. I realized this important fact at the young age of ten. Even though I experienced a "failure" with my first attempt at a solo, I was able to overcome that fear by facing it again and walking through it.

What are your fears? Make a list of them. Say them out loud. When you verbalize your fears, you will often find how ridiculous, inaccurate, or inappropriate they are for your life. Confronting your fears is the equivalent of what parents do when they turn on the lights and look under the bed to dispel the fear of a hidden bogeyman. Shine a bright light on your fears, and watch them fade away or disappear.

A prime example of a limiting fear was when I once needed to make a few simple phone calls to set up interview times for my Internet radio show. I just couldn't do it. I knew in my mind this wasn't difficult, since I'd definitely done more challenging tasks and assignments in my life. So why, then, couldn't I dial the phone? What was holding me back? Why was I so afraid to pick up the phone? I procrastinated for over two weeks and made excuse after excuse for not making the calls. Finally, determined not to fail at this task, I decided to confront the fear head-on.

With a little inner searching, I realized it wasn't making the phone calls that posed the problem. It was making the phone calls while my husband was within earshot. I feared being judged or criticized about my ability to call strangers to book an interview. Now, let's take this a step further. I was afraid he would discover that I was not as confident and competent as I'd always led him to believe. I wanted to make the calls when he wasn't around, so that if I said something stupid, he wouldn't know about it. So in reality, I feared the criticism of someone whose opinion I respect and value. Sometimes when we think we fear one thing, it turns out to be something else that's really the bugaboo.

After discussing this with him (with many emotions coming to the surface), I was able see that one of my biggest challenges in this lifetime was cropping up again — I care way too much what people think about me, both positively and negatively. Once I voiced this fear, I let it go, made the phone calls, and moved on. But not without consciously noting my lesson for future reference; nothing and no one can give me the love of self that I seek. I cannot get it from a career, relationship, family, or material possession. I am all that I need to find this love, and I am the only one who can give it — no one can take it away from me, either.

Remember to speak your fears out loud. Voicing them has tremendous power. When you let them roam around in your mind, they have a tendency to grow into something much bigger than they really are. Once you voice them out loud, you will find the wisdom within you to set them free. When we let our imaginations rule our minds with all the negative possibilities, it is not easy to see the brighter, more positive side to it all. Have courage to live a life that is more important than all the difficulties our fear has created in our minds. Real life is infinitely more important than fear. All successful women have fears; they just know how to walk through them.

Thinking Big

"Our deepest fear is not that we are inadequate. Our deepest fear is that we are powerful beyond measure. It is our light, not our darkness that frightens us most. We ask ourselves, 'Who am I to be brilliant, gorgeous, talented, and famous?' Actually, who are you not to be? You are a child of God. Your playing small does not serve the world. There is nothing enlightened about shrinking so that people won't feel insecure around you. We were born to make manifest the glory of God that is within us. It's not just in some of us; it's in all of us. And when we let our own light shine, we unconsciously give other people permission to do the same. As we are liberated from our own fear, our presence automatically liberates others."
— Marianne Williamson

SOME OF YOU may be able to relate to my personal mental block: believing I am truly powerful, talented, and brilliant, along with all those other wonderful qualities Marianne Williamson talks about, and allowing myself to think big. I knew from the very beginning of my entrepreneurial journey this was a stopping point for me. And I knew I had to overcome it at some point if I ever honestly wanted to make a difference in my life and the lives of others. So imagine my surprise when I realized that I already thought big!

My first business happened without any planning. My life was going in a completely different direction when a simple question changed my life. "Why don't you sell that to other people?" What? Little old, unemployed me? Sell something I created to someone else? Who would want it? I mean, I made it after all, so it's not worth anything. Still, for some reason — probably the nagging by my husband who'd suggested it in the first place — I listed my products for sale in the papers. Someone bought one. And then more people called to see more of them. I made more. Then I sold more.

I told myself, "Hey — I have a business here!" With help from other people (role models, techie people, and support groups), my operation grew from a basement/garage business making just a few thousand per year to over twenty times that total years later. This completely blew my original limiting beliefs out of the water. My business not only grew beyond my imagination but also went global!

Not too long after this, I attended a seminar about exporting to the United States (from Canada), and the speaker asked how many of us already ship products to the States. I raised my hand right away, thinking this was the way everyone did their business. Taking a look around the room, the speaker said, "Only one of you?" What? I had started thinking big, and I didn't even know it. The fact was that everyone in that room had the potential to sell to the States, but something had held them back.

This is a personal mission for me now. I love letting businesses know that they can take their "little local business" out to the global village. That's what is so fabulous about having confidence in yourself and your business. It enables you to think big and shine.

Confidence Gives Voice to Your Passions

WHAT I TRULY love about my own personal journey to confidence is that it taught me that I had the power to put a voice to my passions. And what's more, I gained an understanding for when and where to use my voice for success. I know personally that in times of indecision, it's tempting to look for answers from others rather than taking the risk of listening to your own voice. "Should I go here?" "What do you think?" "Should I do this?" And while it may prove to be valuable to ask a wiser, more experienced person on occasion, or look to your role models for inspiration, there is one person alone who can honestly give you the right answer to any of your questions: You.

Some call it passion, self-confidence, or inner strength. Whatever term you prefer, it's still an internal device that sources outside yourself have virtually nothing to do with what you feel, or what is right or wrong for you. Dig deep within to find your answers. They are there all the time. Listen to your inner voice. It won't steer you in the wrong direction.

I was told once that we all have a purpose or a message to share with the world. This is true, and we need to make the decision to find a way to share that message. What good is having something important to share and then not having it heard by anyone? You have to make noises!

So, following the example of some of my role models, I delved into the world of networking. It was one of those areas that I had absolutely no idea what it was all about or how it could help my business. And for the first few meetings I attended while experimenting with the concept, I found myself experiencing some very similar symptoms to my first solo: sweaty hands, fast-beating heart, and a blank mind.

I wondered why I was putting myself through these emotions again. Then it dawned on me: These women are here to support each other, hear each other, and help each other become truly successful. Amazing! They actually want to hear my message. I've found a place to share my message!

Networking is a fabulous tool for women in business. It suits our style of communication. And running a business is entirely about communicating your message to other people who want or need to hear it. When you find the group that fits you and your business and your personal style, it can also really help to build your confidence. Not only that, but I also found an immense pool of experts to help me get my message out.

POWEr in Numbers

"I was always looking outside myself for strength and confidence, but it comes from within. It is there all the time."
— Anna Freud

THIS EXPERIENCE HELPED me to realize how I can voice my passions, tap into my networking source of experts, and reach the global village 24-7. I studied the art and skill of broadcasting early on, just because there was that inner desire to reach more and more people with my messages. So Internet radio was a natural match for me when I discovered it online.

Even when I might have had those sweaty-palm moments hosting my first shows, I gained confidence through the expertise and resources of others. This made me feel good because I also grew to realize that I had forged a new path for myself that I hadn't thought of before. I love inspiring others through the lessons I've learned on the way to confidence.

On a side note, I was selected to do the solo after my audition the following year, when I was eleven. I put myself in the spotlight, hands sweating, heart beating fast, and opened my mouth and — wham! I nailed it. A true success. I actually got a standing ovation, and that same feeling

of success pushes my business today. Risks, the spotli;
giving words to my passions taught me that I have an i
am here to learn, to teach, and to inspire.

May you gain confidence in yourself, your iae.,
your business.

About

Rose-Anne

Kumpunen

ROSE-ANNE IS a women's activist, a mom of two, a documentary film
producer, and an Internet entrepreneur with over twenty websites offering
advice and information about food, nutrition, alternative health, and holistic
beauty. She is also the vice-president of Kristian Industries and KRIN
communications. Her passion is helping women make permanent and
positive changes in money, mind, body, and soul. She currently educates
through documentaries, online magazines, public speaking, and writing, and
she continues to host a weekly Internet radio talk show: Real Life Radio.
As director for the Power of Women Exchange, Bay of Quinte chapter, Rose-
Anne encourages women in business to network, to expand their markets,
and to grow their businesses in the global village. She lives with her family on
thirty-six acres in beautiful Quinte West, Ontario.

Please visit Rose-Anne at
www.reallifechanges.com

Chapter XI

CONFIDENCE IS CONTAGIOUS

BY AMANDA WILLETT

CONFIDENCE IS CONTAGIOUS
by Amanda Willett

"One of the greatest powers in the universe is the individual power of choice, and the most powerful choices are positive ones."
— Fredrick Mann

There comes a time in your life when you realize that if you stand still, you will remain at this point forever. As the masters of our own souls, we as women have the ability to devise the blueprint to make it happen. My personal journey of self-discovery has taught me the importance of self-confidence and attitude in realizing your dreams and maximizing your potential. When you learn to change your attitude to one of empowerment, you're able to open the door to endless possibilities, and that revelation will change your life.

For years, I have been giving people the wrong impression of who I am as a person. Our attitudes are formed by experience. As an only child, I felt a great deal of pressure to be perfect. Constantly seeking approval, when my mother said, "We want only the best for you," I interpreted it as, "We really want the best from you." Any mistake or shortcoming was the end of the world to me. I was lucky to have parents who truly loved me and believed in me, but, being stubborn and unable to see, I decided my life didn't belong to them. I ran away from home at the age of fifteen in search of my identity. As a mother at the age of eighteen, I chose the hard road in life. I felt like a failure (in my own eyes) to all who loved me.

Enduring many hardships, I suffered from anxiety and depression. During my teenage years and even into my twenties, I spent a lot of time struggling with who I was. I faced the dilemma of indecision as to what to do with my life. I lacked the ability to define what success meant for me, and I chose to spend time around others who were poor influences. My ambitions and dreams were compromised by my negative self-induced energy. I had no self-control and was pessimistic and unable to let go of the baggage I was carting around. When situations or challenges presented themselves, I would draw from this baggage. This influenced my ability to make decisions and ultimately to believe in my abilities to succeed. I lacked the confidence required to reach my potential and achieve my desires.

Stepping Stones

OUR ATTITUDES COMPRISE our second face to the world; the face cannot fail to eventually disclose the truth about the inner you. Learning to love yourself and believing in your abilities is a stepping stone in achieving your positive perspective. It is your outlook on life that directs your inner energy towards outer appearance and outcome. Most of us are paralyzed by fear of making the wrong choice and by not choosing to use the power within us at all. We choose to stay quietly within the boundaries someone else has defined for us. As we abandon the thought of exploring our dreams, the power fades away. These attitudes shape our lack of confidence and ability to use our hidden talents.

We've all had experiences at some point in our lives that have left us jaded. As children, we're taught from a very young age to look outside ourselves for validation. We are instilled with the fear of nonconformity, worried we will not measure up to the status quo and wanting to be accepted and fit in, even if it means doing things we may not value. The most important lesson we should learn from a young age is that we are all unique individuals capable of great things. We need to become our best selves, not an imitation of someone else. Only then can you learn to stop basing your self-worth on what others may think of you.

Creativity will move you past adversity, with beauty, confidence, and absolute bliss. Role models are described as those individuals whom we "aspire" to be, and who provide strong and achievable targets we follow in pursuit of our careers or personal endeavours. At some point in our lives, we've come across someone we wished to become. Oprah Winfrey, Life magazine's most influential woman, continues to be an inspiration to the masses. Many women can relate to her. She rose from a poverty-stricken childhood, suffered abuse, overcame depression, struggled with weight gain, and became one of the most successful women of all time. This woman is truly the "real deal" and one of my greatest inspirations.

An important aspect for women is to feel good about ourselves and be in tune with our personalities. When you are able to become comfortable and confident with whom you are, anything is possible. Maya Angelou, American poet, memoirist, actress, and important figure in the American Civil Rights movement is one of the most honoured writers of her generation, earning an extended list of honours and awards. She, too, endured poverty, abuse, and hardship growing up. Nevertheless, she was able to survive and define herself in terms of being a black woman. Her poetry and autobiographies are about individual strength and the ability to overcome. One of my favourite poems by her is called Phenomenal Woman. Understanding the beauty of all women, her words speak of the confidence and power she owns. She is a remarkable Renaissance woman and someone who has truly inspired my life.

Find Your Purpose

DISCOVERING WHO YOU are and finding your purpose is an exhilarating experience, but it takes time, trial, and error to listen to the call. Once you understand success as a state of mind and not just an outcome, you are able to have a full sense of value for life and what you want to do with it. In my thirties, I reflected on my life: what I had, and mostly hadn't, done or achieved. I needed a change. Having played many roles — the nurturer, mother, wife, and rescuer to many — for once in my life, I wanted it to be about me. Living my life trying to please everyone in it, I had denied myself what would make me fulfilled and happy.

My search within allowed me to get in touch with my own emotions. I dissected my levels of unhappiness. I was stuck in a male-dominated job. The money was good, but I didn't feel valued. Day after day, I hid under a hardhat, wearing coveralls and work boots. Unable to express my feminine side, I wasn't doing a job I loved and didn't feel I was able to achieve my best self. My position didn't symbolize who I was as a woman. Working for a large corporation, I was surrounded by negativity and stress. The hours I worked were inhumane, and I soon realized it was affecting my health and well-being. I was unable to find balance in any part of my life. Everything I loved to do had gone by the wayside.

My entrepreneurial spirit led me to realize I was determined to find and play a rewarding role. I wanted to be a successful leader, a woman with confidence, and someone who was able to make a difference. I started to read inspirational books and stories of other women who discovered their niche. Seeking assistance from others, I was beginning to see the silver lining. It was time to step out of my comfort zone and think outside the box. When I discovered my passion, I realized my inner map had been there all along, waiting to be explored. The answer was always within, and it was time for me to stop standing still. I needed to become a creator rather than a creature of my circumstances.

For a year I worked on a plan in order to reach my goals. I practiced silencing my inner critic and pictured myself happy. The words "I can't" were replaced with "I will." I learned many successful people have at some point failed miserably. The difference is they made a choice to use the experiences to better themselves and become stronger. I held onto the belief that I could do anything I put my mind to. Many laughed, shamed me, and told me I was better off staying put. These individuals were filled with fear and unable to let go of outgrown beliefs and values. People will challenge your choices, and some may not accept your changes. Change is inevitable, and learning to embrace it has been an important part of reclaiming my identity.

My vision of change became more concrete by developing a business plan. My journey to become who I was always destined to be, a woman of strength, compassion, and inner beauty, enabled me to pursue my passion. During this period my "aha" moment was born along with my new company — Beyond Diva Image Consulting Services. As a model, dancer, and beauty contestant, my love affair with fashion and beauty and a desire to look good at all times began at an early age. Friday was my favourite day, as my mom and I always went shopping. I spent time sketching drawings of clothing and dreamt of becoming a fashion designer. Image was a form of expression for me, and as a teenager I discovered I liked working with people and advising them on what to wear. Dressing up has always been empowering to me. When I was first devising my business plan, I had hopes of opening a boutique full of fabulous clothing. Then I realized I wanted my business to be about more than clothing. I felt the need to teach women how to define their beauty and their creativity. Unleashing the inner goddess comes from owning your own power. Every woman has the right to celebrate life like a diva. There is nothing more beautiful or alluring than a powerful woman! My desire is to coach women on how to gain confidence in order to make an impact on others through appearance and attitude. Beyond Diva specializes in creating confident women, which is the secret to real beauty. I now realize even more the important dynamic of image and how it can help you become a woman of influence.

With the desire to reclaim my identity as a woman, and to redefine the meaning of beauty, the name Beyond Diva was chosen. Most people have no idea what the word "diva" actually means, as it has been used in the wrong context for years. A true diva sees beauty as a state of mind. She's a vital, dynamic beauty; one who wears her sexiness like her second skin. Her distinctive outer appearance reflects who she is inside. She connects with her inner beauty by being truly herself, more of her own unique person. Her vivacious personality captivates our soul through her energy and fortitude. The most attractive of all is her unshakable confidence. She is a divine goddess, one who's reachable yet remarkably untouchable.

If you look good, you're halfway there. My goal is to teach my clients to work with what they have and to look beyond the surface. Beauty is important, but the whole package you present is what ultimately counts. Your gift to create a presence will become unstoppable, and your victory achievable. Coco Chanel once said, "Dress shabbily, and they remember the dress; dress impeccably, and they remember the woman." Life is divine when you look good and feel great.

"Each of us has the right, the possibility, to invent ourselves daily. If a person does not invent herself, she will be invented. So to be bodacious enough to invent ourselves is wise."
— Maya Angelou

The Three Ps

YOU HAVE THE ability to define success for yourself, so own it. During my personal and professional development, I chose to use the three Ps to identify my niche.

- **Passion:** Uncover what excites you, and do what you love. Don't stand still, believe in your abilities and take your life in directions you never imagined.
- **Perseverance:** Refuse to give up, and you can overcome any challenge that presents itself. Develop the ability to turn roadblocks into stepping

stones by learning from your experiences. Recognize and accept your personal limits, but move beyond them.

- **Plan:** Be guided by your goals but not blinded by them. Set realistic objectives, and develop a plan to make them happen. Step up and take action.

The Power of Support

AS A BUSINESS professional, you represent a brand, and the brand is you. Before you even speak a word, most people will size you up by the way you appear. Your image is a direct reflection of how much you like yourself. If you don't look the part and if you lack confidence in your ability, so will others. The opportunity may become lost. Perception is people's reality, and appearance can create credibility. So how do you make your own luck? By becoming a person of influence and using your attitude, your greatest asset. Creating a strong presence and making it memorable is your secret weapon to getting what you want out of life.

"I believe luck is preparation meeting opportunity."
— Oprah Winfrey

Each of us can have real success and significance by extending our talents, time, and resources to others and by building character in ourselves. Networking is the perfect platform for making powerful connections. People are your greatest asset, so actively seek the advice and expertise you need. When you cultivate a network, the opportunities are endless. If you decide to become engaged with others to deliver on a common goal, success will find you. Choosing to serve others in your network can boost each other's businesses and personal lives. Helping others in your network is paramount to receiving a stream of good things flowing back to you. Learn to study the actions of your connections — others who have built their destinies before you. By surrounding yourself with positive people, you will be able to change your attitude and your life. A supportive circle of influence will make life's journey much more rich and rewarding, not to mention fun.

"I've always believed one woman's success can only help another woman's success."
— Gloria Vanderbilt

I FOUND THIS out when I joined POWE, a wonderful support group of women who want to make a difference in the world and strive to help each other succeed. POWE provides the tools necessary to enrich your life and shape your destiny. People come into your life for a reason. You have to be willing to grab opportunities when they present themselves. Every human encounter is a chance to succeed, learn, and grow. We all know people who seem to have it all, who appear to have spent a lifetime "getting lucky." You can too, by following these key tips to becoming your own "designer label," enabling you to make a lasting impression on all those within your sphere of influence:

- Develop a winning attitude! Identify what you value. Smile and show enthusiasm. People will be attracted to your beauty and will want to be in your company.

- Be distinctive, stand out, and become untouchable by identifying what makes you unique.

- Presence means so much more than being present! Identify how you want to be perceived.

- Become knowledgeable! Set yourself up as an expert, and identify your specialty.

- It's not what you say; it's how you say it! Learn to become a confident speaker. When you become confident in what you say, people will become confident in your abilities.

- Dress for success! Understanding what to wear for your body type and personality will give you all the confidence you need to look the part. Learn the power of colour and how to make the most of what you've got.

- Build a Network! Take advantage of everyday opportunities to meet people. Volunteer your services, and participate actively in organizations. Make yourself visible.

- Embrace opportunity! Be open to life's "you never know" possibilities. Recognize them when they are presented, and seize them.

- Embrace change! Learn to see the positive in everything you do. Turn roadblocks into stepping stones.

NOW THAT I'M thirty-five, I am finally comfortable in my own skin. I've reclaimed my identity and developed a renewed sense of confidence. I've incorporated many things and practices into my daily regime in order to make this happen. I choose to seek my courage through my daughter's eyes. I pray she will be guided by a positive circle of influence, giving her inspiration to persevere through the challenges of womanhood. My circle of influence has taught me to stop judging myself and others. I've discovered my strengths and choose to work on my flaws. Every day, I tell myself three things I'm happy for. Along with this, every day I read a Buddhist prayer on happiness. Take time to focus on your essential self, because it's crucial to your success. Meditation lets us observe our minds and, through regular practice, allows us to begin to spot the triggers that lead to fear. Yoga and Buddhism have great abilities to assist you in becoming aware of your feelings, and I encourage you to explore those teachings.

Every day, I practice gratitude by learning to be thankful for all the supportive people in my life. I thank my mom for unconditional love no matter what, my dad for knowing how to enjoy life and live in the moment, my grandmothers for believing in me, and my daughter for making me proud and showing her strength as a young woman — without her, my journey would be incomplete. I'm grateful to my husband for embracing change and rising above fear, and to my closest friends who have walked with me and sometimes carried me through the darkest times.

As the law of attraction states, what you focus on, you attract into your life. When you focus on being grateful for what you have, you attract what you want. I have developed a dream board for my future. It is a reflection of my goals, inspirations, dreams, and desires. It is a map of new beginnings, my longing for personal growth, and the wish to discover and try new things. My grandma always told me, "It's your faith that makes you stronger; you just have to fuel it." As she watches over me, I choose to live passionately with confidence and the belief I can accomplish great things. We all have the ability to become influential women. Build your circle of influence, and choose a positive network of support. When a woman feels beautiful, it shows, and when she exudes confidence, it's contagious! Celebrate womanhood. Choose to live every day with the strength of a spirited attitude toward life. It's about finding who you are, then using who you are and what you do to serve yourself and others. As you fuel the flame of your burning desire, listen to your inner voice for direction. With the power to believe, you will achieve and success will find you.

About Amanda Willett

WITH THE DESIRE to reclaim her identity as a woman and to redefine the meaning of beauty, Amanda Willett is now the founder of a brand new company: Beyond Diva Image Consulting Services. Amanda is a woman of strength and compassion — a diva with a heart and an impeccable sense of style. As an image coach, mentor, and speaker, Amanda empowers women to look beyond the surface, enabling them to reveal both their inner and outer beauty. Her goal is to help women achieve their personal best by helping them build their confidence and self-esteem through an awareness of the impression that is made by personal appearance.

Amanda has a degree in business administration with a major in human resource management and has worn many hats in both the public and private sector. Recently, she completed her studies in New York City at the NY Image Resource Centre. A skilled personal shopper and wardrobe consultant, Amanda's fashion sense and awareness of the importance of body type complement her services to create the perfect look every time. Beyond Diva Image Consulting Services is set to launch in 2009 in Durham Region. As a professional image consultant, Amanda's workshops take women on a personal journey of discovering their essential selves, designed to empower them with the ability to make a lasting, memorable impression. Amanda's aim is to become a life coach inspiring others to live out their dreams.

Your image speaks before you do!

Please visit Amanda at
www.bdimageservices.com

Chapter XII

BE A WILD DAISY

BY HEATHER PARDON

Chapter XII

BE A WILD DAISY
by Heather Pardon

"To walk through fields of pure white daisies on a summer's day is to know an indescribable serenity."
— Marie Sperka

Wild daisies are an intriguing flower. They are happy wanderers, adapting well to living in a variety of environments and quietly making a home where other flowers could not thrive. Frequently found lining roadsides, inhospitable country fields, and rock-strewn meadows, this vibrant flower with its dainty, snow-white petals and soft golden centre makes an indelible impact on the landscape. They bloom luxuriantly and bring joy to an entire meadow or add accent to a home garden.

These beautiful flowers also spread quickly and easily. Once ripe seeds are sown, they germinate quickly and make small blooming plants the following year. The wild daisy also self-sows quite readily, producing new seedlings that bring forth more daisies. It knows the wisdom of nurturing its own seeds and fostering new growth in other plants. It knows that this is how luscious meadows are created. There's a lot we can learn from this humble little flower.

I wasn't always aware of the beauty, power, and nature of a wild daisy. Nor how being more like a wild daisy, both personally and professionally, could truly change my life and business. This flower has been a favourite through the years of a fellow gardener — a friend and colleague — who has helped bring it to my attention and teach me about its wonderful qualities.

My story is literally one of a seed that became a wild daisy. Applying the same principles to your life will help you become a wild daisy too.

Always an avid cyclist, I purchased my first road bike over twenty-five years ago. I was immediately hooked on the sport, spending hours riding the side roads around my family home in Whitby, Ontario. I loved the feeling of freedom that cycling brings: the wind against my face, being able to propel myself to destinations that I'd previously thought were accessible only by car.

I remained a "roadie," as cyclists are called, for a few more years until I heard about something called mountain biking, which involves riding on dirt-packed trails through the woods. Intrigued enough by the sound of an exciting new challenge, I gave it a try and bought a shiny new mountain bike and found a couple of friends who happily joined me on the trails.

Unexpected Opportunities

A COUPLE OF years later, I received a letter in the mail from a woman named Michelle Ward who had decided to create a women-only mountain bike community called FlyGurlz. She was offering women the chance to get together for rides and friendship in what was then quite a male-dominated sport. I thought it sounded like a fantastic idea, so I readily signed up. At the time, I was open to the fun of the experience; I had no idea what a huge impact being a part of FlyGurlz would have on my life as the years moved on.

How many times in life have you turned down opportunities because you didn't know exactly how they were going to turn out? Or who you were going to meet? Or what might happen? Oftentimes, we turn down opportunities because we can't see the end result. We want to know that if we invest in something, however big or small, we'll see some kind of result. My advice is to remain open to new experiences, not the outcome, and to let the seed develop. And such was my case with FlyGurlz, which turned out to be the seed of a life-changing experience. My work as a gardener began.

FlyGurlz began as a small group of about twelve women but grew quickly through the years. One year, a woman named Tracy joined the team. Tracy was an ebullient and fun-loving woman who was also a great mountain biker. She competed in twenty-four-hour solo mountain bike races, which meant she rode her bike, non-stop, by herself, around a lapped course for twenty-four hours. It's a tough event, and not for the faint of heart. Until that point, I viewed myself as a rather average cyclist, never deeply questioning my abilities. I told myself many times that I would never and could never do a solo twenty-four-hour race. That it was something that was just not possible. And as Henry Ford once said, *"Whether you believe you can or can't, you are right."*

Apparently, Tracy thought differently. She suggested that I give this solo race a try. Actually, "lobbied" would be a better word, for she never gave up on talking to me about the idea. And so I eventually relented, and two years later found myself standing at the starting line of my first twenty-four-hour solo race.

Oftentimes, others see potential within us or opportunities for us that we cannot see or acknowledge ourselves. We are blinded by our own limited vision of how we see ourselves and what might be possible. What did Tracy see that I couldn't? What did she know that I didn't? She saw an opportunity for me, a possibility, and also shared her own potential. Then she planted and nurtured the seed of an idea in me to do the event. I may not have made it to the starting line had it not been for her kind-hearted prodding.

Think of friends, family, and colleagues in your circle. Are you actively planting seeds in them? Recognizing opportunities that they might not see? And nurturing their potential? That is what wild daisies do. They sow and nurture other seeds. They foster new growth in other daisies. They know that to enjoy the beauty of a meadow, they must freely give of themselves. What could you do to help expand the meadow today? What seeds could you be busy sowing in others?

The summer after I finished my first twenty-four-hour race (yes, there was more than one!), I entered into what was one of the most challenging times of my life on a personal level. And I dearly needed a holiday. I was at a mountain bike race that summer where I met a woman named Nancy who told me she was planning a trip to a race in Whistler, British Columbia, with two other FlyGurlz team members. She wondered if I would like to join them. Did I dare?

Let Your Heart Guide You

WITH FINANCES TIGHT, I probably should not have gone on the trip. I barely knew any of these other girls and was looking at spending a week in close quarters with them. And while I don't live my life according to what I find inside fortune cookies, I do, however, have one stuck on my computer screen, which reads, "Let your heart guide you." And in this case, I did. My heart told me to go, and off to Whistler I went.

That is what wild daisies do. They let the winds of nature guide them and trust that it will not lead them astray. Erin, Jenn, Nancy, and I quickly became good friends and shared many laughs and adventures on the trip. I often liken their friendship to the mountain-biking version of Sex and the City, put on fast forward. It was on a drive up to Whistler from Vancouver that we decided to give each other nicknames for the trip. We began a brainstorming exercise, writing down any words that appeared on roadside signs. Somewhere along the highway there was a Daisy Creek, and thus my nickname became Daisy.

I happily returned home with my new "Daisy" identity, which added a much-needed element of fun to my life. I was struggling at the time and unhappy in my job, with no clear vision as to where to go. Then one day, my friend Jackie suggested that I should open a bed and breakfast. The thought had never crossed my mind before, yet now that she had planted the seed in my mind, I considered the possibility. The more I thought about it, the more dissatisfaction I felt in my current job. This helped with the realization that I needed to do work that fuelled my soul.

There is an essential point not to be missed here. And that is, you must listen to and pay attention to ideas and opportunities that are presented by others. Particularly when you are in the midst of searching for answers or solutions to a problem you may be encountering. Are you currently looking for new business opportunities? Wondering which way to go in life? Trying to decide how to grow your income? It is absolutely essential that you pay attention to any ideas or suggestions that others present to you at those times, as they may be just the seed of an opportunity or a kernel of an idea that you are looking for. Don't be so quick to dismiss them; they may be just what you need. Perhaps others can see a talent or a need in you that you haven't yet recognized.

The possibility of opening a bed and breakfast wouldn't leave my mind. It was the seed of an idea, it was sprouting, and I realized that I needed to act upon and nurture it. At the time, two friends had also given me a waffle maker that I was quickly becoming addicted to. I realized that unless I wished to balloon in weight, I needed to share my new love of waffles with others. I now had the idea for the bed and breakfast as well as the waffle maker. It was time to make my move!

How many times do we miss opportunities in life or limit ourselves by not acting upon those lingering thoughts and ideas that live within our hearts? It is our responsibility to become aware of and nurture those lingering thoughts or seeds of possibility within ourselves, as well as in others. It is taking action on these possibilities that will lead us in directions above and beyond what we may have ever imagined for ourselves. The seed was planted, and now it was time for the daisy to grow.

On several occasions, I'm asked how I came about the name for my business. Reflecting back on the path that led me to the opening of the B&B, I knew I wanted to incorporate the name "Daisy" as a tribute to the people who'd helped nurture the seeds of my journey. And so, A Wild Daisy Bed and Breakfast was born. A few months later, I also launched my personal training business, Wild Daisy Fitness.

I feel a huge sense of gratitude for the people who planted and nurtured the seeds within me, who nurtured their own seeds and potential, and who saw possibilities that I couldn't see in myself. Stop yourself here and take some time for your own reflection. Consider where you are right now in your career, work, love, family, or any other area you'd like to include. Now look back and make a list of five events, suggestions, ideas, or people that have had an impact on you, what you've become right now, what you've achieved or how they influenced a particular outcome or transformed your life. The events may be positive, such as getting married, or they may be negative, such as losing a job.

Many times, events in our lives may turn out quite differently than they initially appeared. For example, I was once demoted from a part-time position at a local retailer. I didn't wish to stay in the job, so a friend suggested that I apply at another store nearby. A few months after being hired, I was asked to speak at their annual "women only" evening as one of the keynote motivational speakers. As a result of speaking at that event, I realized how much I enjoyed public speaking and wished to continue to share my message to help others. So you see, sometimes bad things happen for a good reason. I am thankful that I listened to my friend's suggestion about where to apply for another job, as that experience opened new doors of opportunities and possibilities.

Watch Your Seeds Grow

What events or people have been key for you? Once you have your list, take a moment to express appreciation and gratitude for the opportunities they have provided. When I experience this, I call or write that person to thank them directly, to let them know how their words or suggestions impacted me. You may wish to do the same. It has a huge impact on others to know that they've made a difference to you. Any gardener knows the joys of watching their seeds grow.

Strive to become more aware, and pay attention to the opportunities or to the seeds that present in your own life. Or that you present in the lives of others. For the next week, keep an "Opportunity Journal" or what you also may wish to call your "Wild Daisy Journal." On one side of the page, write down each time someone makes a suggestion to you or gives you an idea. You could call this your "Seeds in My Garden" list. How will you know these? I have noticed in my experience that they may sound like this: "You should give so and so a call…," "This is a great book, I think you'd enjoy it…," "Have you ever thought of …?" or "Could I suggest that…?" These kinds of statements may present hidden opportunities that we may not yet have considered.

On the other side of the page, keep a list of the seeds you have sown in those around you. The ideas, thoughts, or suggestions you have given others. You may wish to call this your "Planting Seeds for Others" list. At the end of the week, consider how many seeds were in your garden. Do you have a long list or a short list? How many did you act upon? How did you feel about some of them? Are you excited or indifferent? How many seeds did you plant for your friends or colleagues? Do this exercise to begin building an awareness of the opportunities and potential that resides within yourself and within those around you. Once you have developed that awareness, you can begin to look at your list and choose which seeds you'd like to act upon. If you're excited about one or more of the seeds on your list, chances are those are the seeds you will want to nurture.

A wild daisy knows its responsibility in sharing and spreading its seeds. It knows that its purpose in life is to nurture its own seeds and growth, to share its life, and to foster growth beyond itself. It knows that what it sows will grow and multiply in beautiful magnitude. To realize our own potential and to help others realize theirs is to know an indescribable joy, happiness, and love of life and have an appreciation for our life's work. And to know what it is to be a wild daisy.

About

Heather

Pardon

HEATHER is a life change coach, certified personal trainer, public speaker, author of I Like My Eggs Sunny Side Up, and former chef who also operates a bed and breakfast in Ottawa, Ontario. Heather's mission in her work is to help others grow the seeds of potential within themselves through fitness, coaching, and self-examination. Her secret to success lies in doing work that fuels her soul, with her goal being to help fuel the souls of others. Her training and background includes a Bachelor of Commerce, chef's training certificate, wellness and lifestyle management certificate, CanFitPro personal trainer specialist, and certified life coach for fitness professionals.

Please visit Heather at
www.wilddaisy.ca or email heather@wilddaisy.ca

Chapter XIII

ON BACON AND EGGS, BOATS
AND WAVES: COMMITMENT, FEAR,
AND CHANGE
BY LIANNE HARRIS RACIOPPO

Chapter XIII

ON BACON AND EGGS, BOATS AND WAVES:
COMMITMENT, FEAR, AND CHANGE
by Lianne Harris Racioppo

One day you may wake up with a stomach-churning realization that fear has been — and may likely still be — dominating your life. Whether in our personal lives or business experiences, there may have been previous preconditioned fears about any reason for "going out on your own." We buckle to these fears by the "what if" mindset. *What if I fail? What if they laugh? What if I get in too deep?* Fear about being an entrepreneur is not unfounded. Well-meaning friends and family may steer you off the idea, critics may be secretly envious, and no one seems to understand your vision. Entrepreneurship is not for the faint of heart. With freedom comes a price. You are solely responsible for the will, drive, energy, time, and outcome of your life. You are free to eat, and equally free to starve. You're challenged on all fronts — mentally, emotionally, creatively. You will stretch and grow and tap your own resources you never knew existed. You live on your own terms, and that's worth much. That's why we do it. I'd like to share with you a bit about my life and what I've learned about commitment, fear, and change.

Bacon and Eggs: Commitment

SITTING DOWN WITH Bruce, my business advisor, he pointedly asked me to visualize a plate of bacon and eggs in front of me. He asked me, with respect to my business, which one I was, the eggs or the bacon? I didn't know what he meant. With a glint in his eye, he replied, "The chicken was *involved* in the making of the breakfast, but the bacon was *committed.*"

So I sat there thinking. Was I a chicken or was I bacon? There were a few times I distinctly recalled being bacon — the day I signed my first store lease, the day I cleared out my bank account for my first serious business project, and the day I put my house up for collateral. Those were bacon days — serious commitment. Was I fearful then? I was certainly anxious, I had trepidation, all my processes were trying to hone into whether I had calculated my product and my market correctly. Yet one can have all of these emotions and still know it is right. There is no stupor of thought — just that assuring passionate desire to plough ahead. Looking back, many of the most important decisions were based on gut reaction.

In the life cycle of business, there were times I was the chicken: distracted, forlorn, weary, and terrified of what to do next and not knowing whether I could effect change fast enough to make a difference.

Who, at times in business, thinks they can be the egg and get all the "good stuff" with partial involvement? Involved here, involved there, dropping a few eggs for this breakfast or that one, and if it broke, no matter. Living safe, to be sure and in a comfortable position to stand up and leave at any point to drop eggs on another breakfast plate. Involved in the process, but not committed.

Who, more often than not, trembles at the thought of being the bacon? In this situation, there is no going back for that little pig — he was committed to that breakfast, committed to being an essential part of that platter. He was prepared to put much more on the line than the chicken — safety, security, everything he could muster.

Now, please don't misunderstand me, I'm certainly not suggesting that anyone necessarily give up their life for a business as our little porker did for breakfast, but the fact remains that fear to commit to your goal, passion, dream, personal freedom, and peace of mind will give you a life in which you are merely involved. Fear-based decisions shape the qualities and character of ourselves and dictate our life's dreams, goals, and happiness.

Build Your Boat to Leave the Harbour: Fear

YOUR CURRENT FEARS may be shadowed by past fears about pleasing, or appeasing, everyone — except yourself. Perhaps you were afraid you might fail, or displease or shock those people whose opinions you value. It is this day you realize that you have put yourself, and your needs, on permanent hold.

What are these fears?

- Fear of losing control
- Fear of humiliation
- Fear of pain or punishment
- Fear of rejection
- Fear of responsibility
- Fear of failure

Why the fear?

1. Decisions were made because you're scared to death about what might happen if you don't take the safe way out. You'll take what you ***don't*** want rather than what you ***do*** want. You are ***afraid*** you might not get what you really want and are ***afraid*** how much that would hurt.

2. You're afraid if you don't settle for the bird in the hand, there may be none in the bush. You ***deny*** yourself what you really want because you're ***afraid*** to fail and have other people say, "I told you so!"

3. Rather than standing alone or having to fight for what you truly wanted, you let others influence you, telling you what you should like, want, or do. You deny yourself because it's probably for the "best." After all, no one wants or has time to get tangled up in your wild ideas! You're ***afraid*** of imposition.

Fear-based "personal cop-outs" mean paralysis and they put you into a zone (or rut) that is safe and predictable but frustrating because you are wasting precious time in your life, again working for what you ***don't*** want instead of what you ***do*** want.

Have you ever had any of what I like to call "bogeyman fears" specific to business?

1. **Feeling Fake:** Many women fear going into business because they feel "fake." "Who am I to run a business?" "I have no contacts." "I have no idea where to begin." This, for one, may be the fear of responsibility.

2. **What You Fear, You Create:** Fear-dominated decisions can be so powerful that what you actually create is the thing you fear and dread. "What if I lose everything?" "What if I sink myself and my family?" This is fear of humiliation. If you obsess about a negative end result, you may become so attuned to looking for these negative signs that this distraction makes it so that nothing but the negative is possible.

3.   **Fear of Change:** Fear of change in business can really be a summation of many other fears. "What will I do if it doesn't work?" "What if I lose them as a client?" "What if I can't win them back?" There are many fears here, but typically they are fear of rejection, fear of pain, and fear of losing control. You may feel that you are starting over or that you are being perceived differently than what was before comfortable or well understood.

A boat was made to leave its moorings. Deciding to fearlessly commit is not selfishness or recklessness; it is about being your "True You." Your "True You" is found at the core of your being and is the summation of your unique skills, interests, talents, insights, wisdom, strengths, and values, all of which need expression. Remember, fearless living is passionate, not reckless; it is directional, not irresponsible. So untie your boat from the dock and push away.

In business life, it is natural to experience many of the highs — and many of the lows — that plague anyone in the uncharted waters of entrepreneurship. These may be unscrupulous partners, clients who don't pay, clients who move on, unproductive referrals, products that are not shipped or have perished, orders that are not filled, or supply lines that dry up. You will likely confront every kind of fear within business — fear of failure, of humiliation, of loss of control, of pain, of responsibility — and guess what? You'll survive. You won't die. Mistakes and failures are really a form of paid tuition into the entrepreneurial school of experience. What is the worst that will happen? You dust yourself off and simply go at it again!

Many of us entrepreneurs have skills that can never be wholly represented on a job application form — tenacity, for one. And, like running a fine-tooth comb over your body, you must look minutely for any clue, any hint of what talents, ideas, or inspirations might have been overlooked before.

Now set your course — and sail your boat out of the bay!

Uncharted Waters: Change

"Adapt or perish, now as ever, is nature's inexorable imperative."
— H.G. Wells

WINDS BLOW THIS way and that, sometimes upsetting our course and making for choppy waters. When business winds blow, new weather patterns develop: trends, phases, economics, communications, new products, new distractions, modes of doing business, changes in client base, diminishing client base, wrong client base, and all sorts of predicaments. That is what makes business so exciting — and challenging!

One day in your business life, you may likely wake up completely overwhelmed and panic-stricken because you realize you are in way over your head. You went from safely paddling in the shallow end to treading water in the deep. The pressures of business are coming at you fast and furious, and you will feel yourself losing all footing as this undertow threatens to wildly carry you away.

Likely you are not sure how it all happened so quickly. All you know is that you are drowning in life's demands and you are going under fast. You may have lost your confidence and ability to deal with the simplest problems; maybe you are overcome with the sheer number of problems you have or the complexities of the problem. In any case, you feel powerless.

Similarly, the dawning of a new day holds no appeal. You're flat and depressed because nothing is happening with your business. You dread going over your contacts, dread making the calls, bristle at setting up appointments (if you get them), and are resentful around people. Networking groups are a point of annoyance. *"What's the point?" "They don't get it — nobody gets it." "I'm so tired of explaining myself."*

You may feel betrayed by investing so much time and energy into a business that appears to have let you down. On this day, you will wonder where you will get the time, money, brains, energy, or strength to get through. You may ask, *"Who am I faking?" "I don't know what to do...I don't have any answers." "I am beaten, so I just want out."*

When you feel this way, it is time to batten down the hatches and set your sails for another course. Prepare for the day of reinvention and adaptability. Expect it. Prepare for it. Don't apologize for it.

Riding new and often rough waters of change will likely test all your abilities, but that change in direction can often be very rewarding. After all, how did you not know that you were, in fact, heading for a crash course to a deserted island? By setting a new sail, you may be on your way to new vistas and horizons, stopping along the way at interesting and populated islands. How many times have you been faced with a change and asked yourself questions such as these?

1. *Why must I change?* Because nothing in life is static. It is a universal law.

2. *Can I change?* Generally, not only can you change, but also you must. Change is necessary for growth.

3. *How do I change?* With good support and a positive attitude.

4. *What do I need to change?* Perhaps your mindset, your personal look, your business mission, your business material, or your physical space.

5. *Do I change myself, or do I change my customers?* The answer may be both. That will depend upon what you are going after.

6. *Why am I afraid of change?* Usually this is fear of the unknown, but the "unknown" fear is wondering whether you'll be perceived as a failure by clients, rejected by existing clients. You may be afraid of your own sense of losing control or your own sense of humiliation that you "had to change." This is irrational fear at its worst. Turn fear into excitement; turn unwanted change into opportunity.

7. *What do I tell my customer if I'm perceived as changing?* Will I appear unstable? Train your client. They will take the cue from you. Always present change as positive. For example, you're not moving your business to a smaller place, you are choosing to relocate for purposes of client convenience and better atmosphere.

8. *Change means creativity. I'm not creative. I can't imagine what I'm to do next.* Do what you do best, and engage the services of creative people who do what they do best. If that is not feasible, there are many books and online resources to help get the creative juices flowing and to give you ideas. Use the many resources available. Talk to other business people, join networking groups, and share ideas. The more you do, the easier it gets.

9. ***Is changing somehow being deceptive? Are you a liar?*** No, change is inevitable. Every business changes. The Barbie doll was once made in the creator's garage. Is it now? No, the facilities had to change to adapt to market demand. Your business will change too. Expect it. Embrace it. Change may make you feel awkward at first, but is there anything wrong with changing from a child to an adult? No, Every stage will be better than the last to effect progress. You must progress accordingly.

10. ***The Best Change of All:*** Improvement is a form of change. After all, something is getting better and better than what it was before. Things that should always "change" for the better: honesty, integrity, sincere client relationships, and customer service enhancements.

Calmer Water: Networking

TO BE OTHERWISE alone out in the midst of the great blue sea would truly be lonely, daunting, and perhaps unprofitable. Your ship will have a much smoother journey if you listen to and are in communication with others: weather channels, light houses, and other boaters sharing the same waters. These others send warning signals, tell you of upcoming changes, direct you to good waters, or give you tips on a good island to dock. While docked, your fellow boaters might make good finds among the markets and tell you about that as well. Some might even do trade on your behalf. This is like networking within your business.

I realize business is about change. It's about your *adaptability attitude.* Don't be afraid to readjust your sails' direction. Don't be ashamed if you must learn to paddle your emergency life raft, it's okay to stop for a while at a different island than planned. Be fearless and adventurous about when and where you sail your new boat — your entrepreneur***ship*** — a boat that was *made* to leave the harbour and sail!

About

Lianne Harris

Racioppo,

BA, BFA

Business Owner, Author, Teacher, Artist, Designer, Public Speaker, Historian

LIANNE is the owner of Natural Stuff, Inc., dedicated to education and health care, and the parent company of three other companies. Lianne was chosen as one of Toronto's Top Achievers by WOMAD (Women in Advertising). She is the author of historical novels used in gifted programs in the United States and is an exhibiting artist at the Royal Ontario Museum, Roy Thomson Hall, the IDA Gallery, and the Shaw Festival. A resource specialist in education, she has taught over forty-five thousand students. A much sought-after public speaker, Ms. Harris Racioppo has been the keynote speaker at many professional, academic, and organization events. She is an honours graduate of York University, where she studied fine arts, history, and Latin.

Please visit Lianne at
www.ceragemajax.com

Chapter XIV

DIRECT CONNECTIONS
BY MARIANNE FORD

CHAPTER XIV

DIRECT CONNECTIONS
by Marianne Ford

I believe that networking (connecting, talking to people you don't know, developing relationships, whatever you want to call it), is the number one vehicle to personal growth. You have to get out of your comfort zone. You have to get clear on who you are and what you do. You have to speak up and ask for what you want. You have to learn to communicate effectively. You have to be determined. You have to persist, and you have to learn how to positively handle rejection.

When I started in business, I had to learn all of those things. When I look back, however, I realize that I had an unconscious understanding that talking to people was normal. I really never made the connection that what I was doing was networking or building relationships. For instance, at my very first summer job, I knew that my parents were "well connected" and learned very quickly that it's who you *know*. This trend continued on into my careers in the teaching field, in sales, and in the corporate world, and even when I was looking for a new relationship. The question was always, "Who do you know?"

The reality of business today is that if you haven't established great relationships, you may not get the job you want or the new clients your business needs.

When I recently began my speaking business, again, my first question was, "Who do I know?" And then, "Who do I need to know — how do I make those new contacts?"

Women, especially, are natural networkers. We use it to find all kinds of information, including:
- Dentists or doctors
- Where to meet people
- The best restaurant, stylist, shopping, or auto mechanic

- The best teachers or schools
- To raise money
- To get information on just about anything

This is our "everyday" networking. Word of mouth is still, even in this computer age, your greatest connecting tool. The great news is that it is enhanced by all of the Internet resources.

As I've come to realize, what was different for me from most women I have taught or spoken to is that I knew exactly what I wanted. The vision was so clear, that nothing could have deterred me from my goal. I didn't know how I was going to get there, but I was prepared to do whatever it took. There were many times that I had to change the date of goals. I just never changed the goal! I embraced everything I was taught and told to do by the women who preceded me. They had what I wanted, so why reinvent the path? I worked consistently, focused on that vision every day!

You have to:

- Be clear about what you want
- Visualize it
- Practice
- Follow up

Some people's self-esteem and confidence have been battered. They hold back, not speaking up, being terrified of not saying or doing things "right," and their timidity causes them to lose many opportunities for growth. The only way to become a walking billboard for the business you represent and the person you are is through practice. Unfortunately, you need to fall down many times. The learning is not in the "falling" but in the getting up again…and again…and again!

Vision

SO WHY IS it that some can continually push through their fears while others hide behind them?

The reason we persist through these challenges is because our vision and commitment are compelling. When you know exactly what you want, and are willing to commit to do whatever it takes, it doesn't matter what the fear is. You just plough through! Will you win every time? No, but you develop your strength through patience and deliberate focus. That is the compelling force that drove me every day to do whatever it took to get to the top!

So ask yourself, what is your compelling force? It must include such a strong vision that it will propel you to do whatever it takes to reach your goals. A vision *so big* that it stifles fear and gives clear direction! Without vision, networking has no purpose and can be very scary.

Today the energy I exude is one of very high confidence and self-esteem. Many think I was just born this way, but nothing could be further from the truth. I did not speak up, push through my fears, or attract anything or anyone. In my heart, however, I knew there was so much more. There must be a star in there somewhere! I wanted poise, confidence, position, and to win that pink Cadillac! That vision spurred my enthusiasm every day. Your enthusiasm is what draws people to you. It creates your "presence" and allows determination to create the persistence required to succeed and flourish. Also understand that your enthusiasm does not have to be "over the top." Relax into yourself, love what you do, and allow that positive, exciting energy to exude.

So what is your vision? Do you have one? Are you passionate about it? Have you written it down? Have you been very specific in what you want to accomplish? Do you have timelines? How consistent are you in your efforts? Are you willing to do the work required? Are you willing to do it every day? Are you ready to start now? Do you act as if you are already there?

Commitment

YOUR OLD BELIEF-system tapes are constantly rerunning in your mind, creating limiting thoughts and preventing you from attaining success. Stop focusing on these false and limiting beliefs — turn off that internal tape player. The law of attraction says that whatever we focus on, we get more of. Trust this law, and then "act as if" you are already there...wherever "there" is! You must create unwavering positive beliefs about yourself, write them down, and say them out loud daily. Then commit to whatever it takes for as long as it takes.

When my focus was pink Cadillacs, people would always say, somewhat sarcastically, "So, I suppose you have one of those pink cars?" My answer was always, "I sure do...it's out in the driveway!" They'd run to the window expectantly and then say, "But that's a blue Chevette!" I'd look back at them incredulously and say, "It is?"

I visualized every aspect of that car, from the leather seats to the automatic windows to the prestigious hood ornament, until the real one was in the driveway. I acted **as if** I was already driving that beautiful car long before it was actually in the driveway! It boosted my belief that I could do it and gave me pride in what I did. It also gave me the determination to do the necessary work to achieve the goal. It took five years, but the value of what I learned along the way was immeasurable.

Focus

SO MANY WOMEN are trying to run more than one business at a time. How can you give each one of them the time and effort that it needs? In the beginning, it damages your credibility. Pick one goal, and give it everything you've got! It's important to realize that when you try to do and be everything to everyone you become overwhelmed, agitated, and exhausted, and communication breaks down. You're not easy to live with, and business suffers. It's detrimental to all of your relationships — even the one you have with yourself, since you are usually the last person you spend time with. Let go of control, or at least your "perceived" control. People want to do business with people they like who exude positive energy and are fun to be around.

Being present, in the moment, with the activity or person in front of you, seems to be a lost art. Multi-tasking is the mantra of the day, but beware: It is a myth. Your mind can hold only one thought at a time. Don't kid yourself into thinking you are a master at doing several things at once. The fact is that you are just not focused on any one thing, and you are jumping from one thing to another, giving each task a fraction of your attention. At some point, it will wear you down and your effectiveness will dwindle. Slow down, and enjoy the "moments." Once they are gone, they are gone. When your activity level is so high, so frenetic, nothing and no one gets your undivided attention. Here are a few helpful hints:

- Sit down with your family at the dinner table as often as possible. Make this a priority.
- Don't wear your "uniform" (business attire) to dinner, and don't answer the phone.
- Don't be on the phone when your kids or your partner come in the door.
- Don't interrupt a live conversation when your phone rings.
- Have a relaxing bubble bath in the middle of the day.
- Write a journal to capture moods and ideas, and to "download" your thoughts.
- Exercise to relieve stress and maintain good health, physical fitness, and good appearance.
- Stop insisting that you're right. Sometimes you may not be!
- Have a date with your spouse or partner every week, and focus on your relationship.
- Talk less, and listen more.

Norman Vincent Peale said that unless you are in one of the following "states," you're causing grief for yourself or others:

- **Acceptance:** Accept that this is what this moment requires of you, no matter what it is. For example, my tire is flat, it's raining, and I have to wait for help. There is nothing I can do. Or, I'm in a hurry and I'll never make it on time. I have two choices:
  - Accept the situation as is.
  - Get angry and stressed.
- **Enjoyment:** As long as I keep my thoughts in present time, I can actually enjoy doing what I'm doing. I can focus my thoughts on what is in front of me instead of obsessing about where I'd rather be. I hear and process the "moments" that are presented. I can just "be." Teach yourself to do this by stopping the negative self-talk, and enjoy the present moment and the current journey.
- **Enthusiasm:** This is deepened enjoyment that has an "attracting energy" that everyone wants to be around. You have a strong focus and commitment. You enjoy all of the "moments." Your passion for life exudes from every pore!

- **Activity:** Attracting clients is ongoing and forever. There is no networking without creating activity, so get out from behind your desk!

Early in my career, a senior colleague offered to take me "warm chattering" to get leads. Great! She told me to dress up, bring a briefcase, my datebook, a pen, and lots of business cards, and to meet her at the mall. Okay, then! This was going to be easy! Or so I thought.

I looked like a million bucks, carried my husband's brown suitcase (with nothing inside), pen, and cards, and was ready to go! She said, "Great! You go down this side of the mall, and I'll go down the other. Just talk to people and give out your card, and I'll meet you back here in an hour." Then she left me, standing there nonplussed!

My palms became sweaty, my heartbeat doubled, and that total feeling of "I'd rather be anywhere but here" engulfed me. My mouth, which is ordinarily going a mile a minute, ceased to open! Needless to say, I was in the exact same place when she returned, and I'll never forget the look of disappointment she gave me! My self-esteem was not good to begin with, but now I felt like such a failure! If this is how you were supposed to network, it wasn't for me. I just couldn't do it this way!

As I see it, there are three groups of people to talk to:
1. Friends and relatives
2. Acquaintances whom you want to move into the friend category
3. People you don't know whom you want to move to the acquaintance category

Informal networking or talking to people you don't know poses challenges for many of us. I remember walking into parties or casual get-togethers, heading straight for the sidelines, and being the wallflower. Even today, it may not be the most comfortable of situations for me. I'm finding this feeling to be true for many people, not just women.

That's why so many networking communities like POWE have been created. It's much easier now because we can attend a designated networking or connecting lunch or meeting, where starting conversations with "strangers" is expected. You are actually supposed to talk to people you don't know. Now you can build your business on purpose and run your business like a business. Everyone is in the same boat! The only way to build your confidence here is to keep going back and being prepared.

By the time you get to a networking meeting, you've taken a few notes and had disappointments. You are normal; however, now you have to recreate your initial enthusiasm in spite of having suffered some rejection.

It's important to have a thirty-second bio memorized about who you are. Think of it as an "elevator pitch." Make sure your handshake is firm, not bone-crushing and not wimpy. Very aggressive or assertive women's handshakes (the ones that seem to overcompensate for femininity) that almost take you down to one knee are not attractive, and neither is the limp "four-finger wiggle." A handshake should be businesslike, firm and enthusiastic, but not overly forceful. Practice your handshake with someone who will give you honest feedback. Even ask about your approach. What do you need to change to make yourself more approachable? So much is in that first impression — you don't get a second chance to make it.

The relationships you establish are far more important than anything you have to sell. Give to give, don't give to get. Closing the networking deal is easy. Just say, "Why don't we exchange cards?"

Put them on your mailing list, and immediately send a follow-up email saying how nice it was to meet them and giving a short explanation of what you do. Remember, if you fail to follow up, all of your hard "connecting" work will have been wasted.

It's very simple. In business, it's all about the numbers of people you connect with; the more "numbers," the more business.

The Fear Factor

WOMEN ARE PRONE to "visiting" or "helping" versus actually getting names and numbers and following up. We're all so nice! So put us in a setting where we are actually supposed to ask for something for ourselves, and our "fear radar" catapults itself into another universe. So what is this fear?

- Fear of being perceived as pushy
- Fear of rejection
- Fear of not knowing what to say
- Fear of not being good enough
- Fear of people not liking your product
- Fear of what people will say

It's an amazing phenomenon. Often the fear is so overwhelming and it immobilizes so profoundly that we just stand there and do nothing! We go home deflated, and might even say, "I knew that wouldn't work!"

Give some thought to where these fears originated, accept them, and then realize that that was then and this is now. How long are you going to allow things that are not real today stagnate your success? Become conscious of the fact that your limiting beliefs are holding you back, not the present situation.

Your fears about speaking up will always be there until you have talked to so many people that you exude confidence and it becomes second nature. Becoming yourself is the by-product of this journey. Get clear about your fear, face it, and move through it. Write in your journal about it. Make your vision real!

Results

MOMENTUM COMES FROM the actual activity, not the outcome. The great news is that "the more you keep on keeping on," the more your expertise improves. The more experience you gain, the higher your confidence level becomes, and the better the odds! The better the odds, the more money you make!

The Feelings Wheel

REMEMBER HOW EXCITED and enthusiastic you were when you first opened the doors to your new business or started on a new project? How many people did you talk to that week? You could hardly wait to get on the phone or get out the door! Everyone had to have your product! Your vision of success was huge! You knew exactly where you were going!

Somewhere along the line, your enthusiasm started to wane. Maybe you forgot that it's a numbers game. Ya gotta know the odds! Out of one hundred attempts, ten will probably say yes. Unfortunately, you just don't know if it will be the first ten or the last ten!

As you become aware of the ups and downs and how they can often stunt your momentum, you realize there are no shortcuts to feeling comfortable when you are networking. It just takes time and practice. You'll probably have to go through the following Feelings Wheel many times.

Enthusiasm

Anger

Frustration

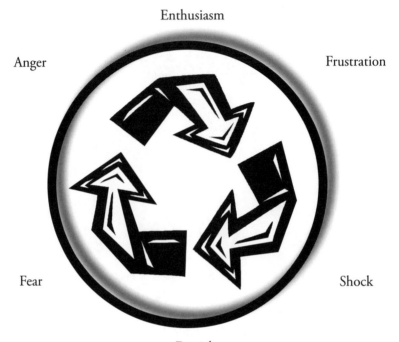

Fear

Shock

Denial

- **Enthusiasm:** Any time you start something new, there is an initial burst of enthusiasm. The promise of success, the money, the support, the new friends, and the personal growth is very exciting. There is nothing that can stop you!
- **Frustration:** Perhaps your order didn't come in, unexpected personal situations have arisen, someone said no, the phone has become more difficult, and even some of your friends and family think you are crazy! But you're still okay and you keep going.
- **Shock:** Someone actually cancelled a booking! Lots of people have said no! Someone even cancelled and didn't tell you! Someone returned a product! You can't believe it! How could this happen? What is the matter with these people? They don't keep their word? Don't they know how important this is?

- **Denial:** The operative words here are "I'm fine." Instead of meeting the obstacle head-on, we choose creative avoidance. We may clean the house, visit friends, go shopping, get another job, take time off...but we're "fine" — we're just not doing any work!
- **Fear:** Unfortunately, if you stay in denial too long, fear starts to show its ugly little head. The phone really does weigh one hundred pounds. It becomes so much more difficult to remain motivated. You become immobilized.
- **Anger:** Who can I blame? It's your recruiter's fault; she talked you into this thing! It's your husband's fault! He's never there when you need him! It's your kids' fault! They just keep you too busy! It's the company's fault! They don't know what they are doing! It's the economy, and you can't control that!

UNTIL WE REALIZE who is actually responsible, this is really a tough place to be, for you and anyone else in your path. Of course, the answer is within you. The good news is that "Anger" is very close to "Enthusiasm" on the wheel!

- **Back to Enthusiasm:** Someone books an appointment. We made the sale, got the new recruit, or won a prize! **Yahoo!** We're back!

You can move around this wheel as quickly as you want, or you can choose to get right off of it, change your thought patterns, and go down a different path. Your "response-ability" will be tested! Awareness of your emotional place on the wheel is the key to your success not only in business but also in life.

It can influence your paycheque dramatically and determine the quality of your relationships. Start noticing where you are on the wheel, and take the steps necessary to get back to enthusiasm as quickly as possible. Do whatever it is you need to do to restart the momentum or rekindle the relationship.

You are totally responsible for living in abundance in every area of your life. Your success and well-being are never about anyone else. It's an "inside" job! The more we understand ourselves, the easier it is to understand others, making us much more effective in everything we do.

It has taken many years to peel back the layers of understanding about myself. I have made many mistakes and fallen many times, but the fact remains that you can't do it alone. Networking is one of the keys to abundance in every area of your life.

experience the adventures and challenges along my
ie tools of my journey in the hopes that they will make
iow that we are all here to help each other through.

About

Marianne

Ford

MARIANNE has been a highly successful speaker and facilitator in the direct sales industry for over twenty-five years. She left her teaching career to earn four pink Cadillacs with Mary Kay Cosmetics. She went on to be the corporate director of sales for two multi-million dollar direct sales companies, plus has become a very popular and highly successful corporate "change" advisor and speaker. Her expertise includes being a licensed facilitator of Stephen Covey's The 7 Habits of Highly Effective People.

She has recorded The Magic Business CDs, which focus on the direct sales business, plus a set called Change Your Thinking, Change Your Life.

Marianne lives with her husband near Toronto, Canada.

Please visit Marianne at
www.marianneford.com

Chapter XV

THE KEEPER INSIDE ME
BY DENISE FRANKLIN

Chapter XV

THE KEEPER INSIDE ME
by Denise Franklin

Since high school, I've worked as a bookkeeper at various levels for small businesses and corporations, both Canadian and American-owned. I've suffered through three rear-end collisions and one rollover accident, and spent many long and tiring days commuting for miles through rush-hour traffic to what I thought would be the *company* I'd retire with, but, like the others, they, too, decided to close their doors. So much for job security! I did, however, quietly thank them and then went on my way. Yet again, I was faced with the difficult reality of finding another job.

What does a forty-eight-year-old woman with a high school education and many years of experience do? Well, I searched for work only to find out that there wasn't much available, and if there was a job, I was either overqualified or under-qualified, or the pay was inadequate.

Fortunately, I received a severance package and had some time to decide what I wanted to do with my life. After some soul searching, I realized the need for a mobile bookkeeping business to help small businesses get on and stay on the right track. In January of 2005, I registered D's Bookkeeping Service, and my journey toward independence began.

For the first year, I barely kept my head above water acquiring clients — some regular, some not. All in all, I was making a decent living. But, there was something missing. I wanted more. What was holding me back? What was keeping me from climbing to that next level in my business? Was it me? Did I lack confidence, self-esteem, or knowledge? Did I have what it would take to be able to increase my business?

So, I took a good, hard look at myself and what I could do to improve. I was slightly overweight, tired, and lacked energy. With encouragement, support, and help from my husband, Ron, not only was I able to lose some weight but I was also able to start eating healthy meals. This gave me the energy and physical vitality to be more productive. I changed my hairstyle and my wardrobe, as well as started to wear flattering makeup. One of the most important changes I made was the incorporation of "Denise Days." On these days, I had either a manicure, pedicure, facial, or massage. Sometimes I had them all on the same day and just celebrated being Denise!

Tanning in the Tropics

I NOW FELT good on the outside, but what about the inside? What about the uncertainties, the lack of confidence and poor self-esteem? Those things are much more difficult to change. The knowledge of my business (which I had gratefully gained over the years) made me a source of information. I was always able to answer any question regarding bookkeeping and small business practices and to talk to people one-on-one, but put me in front of a group, and my brain would go tanning in the tropics somewhere and forget to take me with it. I had no idea what to say. I practiced any chance I got. As a matter of fact, the windshield in my car became my audience, and I didn't have a problem saying anything.

At my first Power of Women Exchange (POWE) meeting, I sat back and observed. After that, I knew this organization was for me, and that networking the POWE way made perfect sense. I wanted to be the one at the front of the room. But how, when I panicked at the very thought of it? So I signed a membership form and walked away saying, "I am going to do this. I can do it." At the next meeting, I stood up in front of everyone with my door prize in hand, proud as a peacock to do my thirty-second infomercial. I had practiced for an entire month in front of my windshield, and was going to be great.

The moment I stood on stage, my brain went tanning again. I stumbled over my own name, said absolutely nothing that I wanted to say, and sat down feeling rather embarrassed. Right there and then, I decided that this one bad time wasn't going to stop me and that the next time I would do better. Some of the ladies in the room, however, wanted to visit with me about bookkeeping and told me how well I did, which was encouraging. This experience did help me realize one important fact: I could always be at the front of the room if I wanted to. I just needed to bring a door prize and continue to practice.

One of the benefits of membership in POWE is that you are automatically a member of all of the chapters. I decided to make one day a week POWE day and attend meetings at as many of the chapters as possible. My most embarrassing moment in POWE was the meeting I attended in Ottawa. All the bigwigs were there. Not knowing this, I stood in front of everyone and offered the door prize again. This time, I had typed my thirty-second infomercial and was going to read it. Now, I know I can multi-task. I can talk on the phone, enter data into a computer, and use an adding machine all while chewing gum and holding a pencil, with no problem at all.

When it was my turn to speak, however, the chapter leader handed me the microphone, and I stood there with my paper in hand and shook. Apparently, I was supposed to hold the microphone and talk at the same time. After what seemed like an eternity, she realized my panic and held the microphone for me. With shaking hands, I read the words that I had so proudly put on paper. I still get up in front of groups and do door prizes, and each time it becomes easier and better.

In the networking circles, I was a little bit better at first, but knew I had to do something to perfect my time at the tables telling everyone what I did and what I was all about. At a few of the meetings, one of the questions that we were asked in the networking circles was to name one of our goals. Well, the one goal I mentioned a few times was that I wanted to be one of the spotlight speakers and get up in front of everyone for ten minutes and tell them what I do.

My chapter leader heard my comment and decided to place my name on the list for the next meeting. I left the meeting that day saying, "I can do this. I am able to accomplish anything I want." Now, let me tell you, my poor windshield heard from me quite a bit that month. When I finished my spotlight time, I thanked Rose-Anne for volunteering me, because deep down I knew that was exactly what I needed in order to get my name out. And yes, I was nervous, but I got through it and even had my audience laughing at one point, and that made me feel good. I've done other ten-minute spotlight talks, while holding a microphone, I might add, and the more I do them, the better I become.

I began setting up vendor tables and displaying information about my business at every chapter meeting I could, and sometimes two meetings a day, to again be in front of everyone. I was able to talk to people one-on-one about their businesses, what I do, and what I could do for them. Doing this put me back in my comfort zone. There are so many activities in POWE to promote your business, from working the registration desk to selling 50/50 tickets, and from doing thirty-second infomercials to ten-minute spotlight talks. The more consistently I stood in front of people, the easier it got and the more business I secured.

Now I volunteer for these positions often and am excited to be the one at the front of the room. I'm also doing Entrepreneur's Workshops aimed toward helping other new and existing entrepreneurs start and maintain their businesses. I am so grateful to POWE for the opportunities it has given me and for what it has made of me.

Inspiring Words

IF I WERE asked about things that have inspired me along the way, I would have to say that my children have inspired me the most. Remember when you were growing up and you were asked, "Who do you want to be when you grow up?" You probably replied, "I want to be just like my mom." Or perhaps, "I want to be just like my dad." Well, now that my children are grown and extremely successful both in life and in business, I want to be just like them!

What they have done and said over the years has helped me become a better person and think better of myself. My oldest daughter, Michelle, helped me start my personal library with books such as *Chicken Soup for the Soul and Wild Succulent Woman*. I continue to add to my library and try to read at least one chapter a day from motivational, fun, and inspiring books. On my fiftieth birthday, I received a phone call from Michelle telling me I could do and say anything I wanted. I'd earned the right. Also, that she couldn't wait to be my age and have the lines of experience that I had. I'd like to take this opportunity to share with you one of the inspirational Mother's Day letters I received from her:

Mommy,

Well, this is my present to you, do you like it?

Over the past couple of weeks, I've been listening to the Mother's Day advertisements on the radio. Given my current feeling on the world and its capitalistic nature, they did little but make me angry. There were three types; I'm sure you're familiar with them.

The first was an attempt to make the child feel guilty about not buying their mother a present. After all the pain and suffering she's been through, from labour to giving up her career to raise you, and all you give her is a card? And then they end by suggesting a present around the hundred-dollar mark.

The other kind was the competitive nature: The present I got Mom is better that the one you got her because mine cost more and it will last longer.

Then there was a "dare-to-be-different" ad on the one and only 1050 CHUM. All it suggested was to call in and request a song to dedicate to your mom on Mother's Day. And I said, "Wow, someone finally gets the point."

However, I know you won't be listening to 1050 CHUM even if I call in and request one. So if I did and if you were listening, I would request "What a Wonderful World" by Roy Orbison (I think he sings it), and I would say that we need to spend more time together in this wonderful world, start walking again and enjoying it. And I would say, "Thanks, Mom, for bringing me into this wonderful world."

I love you lots, 'Chelle

MY YOUNGEST DAUGHTER, Cheryl, has taught me how to have fun in life. As a matter of fact, she's even invited me to join her and her friends on various expeditions, including a trip to Las Vegas. I feel so honoured and important when she calls and asks for my advice. Cheryl was my rebel and always of the opinion that rules were meant to be broken. The day of her wedding, she stood in front of over one hundred people and openly thanked me with these words:

Mom,

If it weren't for you, Mom, we would not be here today. You did so much in the way of planning for the wedding. I don't know what I would have done without you. Throughout my life you have taught me many things: responsibility, loyalty, happiness. I would not be who I am today if it were not for you. When I was young and I would get mad at you, you always used to say, "You may hate me now, but you will thank me someday." Well, Mom, this is the day. You always pushed me and challenged me and made me believe that I could go further in life and achieve better things. When I was annoyed with the co-op department at university and didn't want to apply, it was you that forced me to. You taught me that no matter how big the task, if you put your mind to something, you could achieve it. You taught me to always speak my mind and share my thoughts, as long as I did it in a polite manner and understood that I had to respect other people's thoughts as well. You taught me the true meaning of love and happiness, that life is too short to be unhappy, and we have to live it to its fullest. You taught me that life is not a competition, it is not about winning or who is better than whom, but rather it is about enjoying people and having the most fun you can possibly have while you are here. You taught me responsibilities by making me do my homework before I could play and that there are things in life that we may not like, but we must do. You never once told me any of your problems, but you would stay up all night to listen to mine, and when I would call you at three o'clock in the morning from the university crying, you would listen. You are the strongest woman I know, and I truly hope that one day I can be to my children half the mom that you were to me. I have chosen a fabulous husband, and if it were not for you, I would never have been able to do it.

Later, I was told that she rehearsed her speech a number of times but could not get through it without crying. Well, she did it on her wedding day proudly and with no tears, but there were some shed in the audience. Being a mom was easy with kids as awesome as mine. Their words and actions have inspired me to realize that I am also an incredible, awesome person. I am so grateful for my girls, and although distance is a factor, I cherish the time we have together and they are always with me in my heart.

Make Life a Bit Easier

I'VE PUT A good deal of thought into making my personal and professional life hassle-free. As my business has grown, so have the demands on me and on my time. Many times, I've spent more time trying to remember various tasks and I had "to-do" lists and sticky notes plastered all over my desk. It was bound to happen, and I wasn't even surprised when there were times that I forgot something that I was or wasn't supposed to do. For instance, one day I left to go to a client's office and drove for two and a half hours, only to find out I had forgotten to change the appointment on my calendar after a phone conversation. So I spent (wasted) five hours of driving time, and that was when I realized that things were getting out of hand. I needed to do something about getting organized quickly, before it was too late.

My next stop was to buy a digital voice recorder, which I now rely on as my office assistant. Everything I need to remember gets recorded at the time it happens, and I don't spend any time trying to remember anything. Now those post-it notes stuck all over my desk, computer and day timer are all gone. Every night or first thing in the morning, instead of writing a list of things that I have to do for that day, I simply record it and carry on with my day knowing that when I'm ready to accomplish the next item on my list, all I have to do is listen to the recording instead of searching for a piece of paper.

Also, when I'm at seminars or workshops, I record them instead of trying to take notes or trying to remember what was said, and then I use my driving time to educate myself. This in itself has probably been the best hassle-free, stress-free device that I've ever acquired for my business. Having it allows my mind and thoughts to be more productive. I am now in charge of my thoughts, and I have the power to control them.

I've also applied another technique to my personal life to make it hassle-free: I've learned to block out the negativity in my life. I know that I can't change other people or their opinions, so I either accept them or I move on. I now think of the positive side of things. I arrived at a restroom the other day to find a line of anxious travellers. I said rather loudly, "Yeah, there's a lineup. Good, now I get to socialize!" Inevitably, one of the ladies in the line looked up at me and smiled, and we chatted while we were waiting. I now think of "hot flashes" as "tropical moments" and enjoy them while they last.

I watch, listen, and learn from others who are successful in both business and life. I do what's good for me, not what's good for everyone else. It's time to think about Denise and her wants and needs, I tell myself.

I am grateful for my friends and their encouraging words and their unfailing belief in me. I am fortunate that Ron supports, understands, and respects me for who I am and what I stand for. We take time for ourselves, and, in fact, you'll find us relaxing in the hot tub, me with a glass of wine, almost every night. I laugh more and smile more, and I like to sing little made-up jingles that put me into a happy mode. I stand up straight, I'm proud of who I am, and I love what I do. I look up toward the sky, not down at the ground. I am a Leo, and occasionally I'll come across something that is a pure Leo trait and I think, wow, that is so me. I have a phrase that I carry around in my purse with me, and I repeat it to myself quite often. It says my motto is "I am" and that I am a generous, fun-loving, loyal, and courageous person. I am healthy, beautiful, and energetic. I am now learning how to be me. It isn't whether I can or can't, it's whether I will or won't.

My Recipe for Success:

Ask for help when needed

6–8 hours sleep, accompanied by 3 healthy meals

1 cup each of knowledge, experience, wisdom, and self-esteem

If available, add support, encouragement, and respect

30 minutes each of exercise, reading, and "me" time

Drizzle with chocolate, and add red wine to taste

Top with lots of smiles and confidence, and enjoy

— Denise Franklin

About Denise Franklin

DENISE brings many years of experience to the world of bookkeeping. Having been born in the '50s and becoming a high school graduate in the early '70s has made her one of the generational baby boomers. While doing bookkeeping at various levels, including payroll and collections, she has acquired years of knowledge, enabling her to start her own business to satisfy the needs of her clients. Since high school, she has worked for small businesses, big businesses, and corporations, both American- and Canadian-owned.

Denise, a Certified Bookkeeper and regional developer, is a member of the Institute of Professional Bookkeepers of Canada, the Power of Women Exchange, and the Women's Small Business Network. She is licensed with the City of Quinte West and has been a registered business entity since January of 2005. While operating her business full-time, Denise is also hosting workshops, passing on her knowledge to help other entrepreneurs get on and stay on the right track with their business needs.

Her favourite quote is *"It's not whether you can or can't, it's whether you will or won't."*

Please visit Denise at
www.bookkeepingbyd.com

Chapter XVI

IGNORANCE ON FIRE

BY VALERIE DEE

Chapter XVI

IGNORANCE ON FIRE
by Valerie Dee

It began in the spring of '93, when my brother asked if I'd be interested in a great business opportunity. Normally a skeptic, I nevertheless agreed to take a look, since it was, after all, my brother. At the beginning of our meeting, he drew one circle after another on a piece of paper, all the while telling me how two circles turn into four, which then increase to eight, and again into sixteen, and then to thirty-two, and so on, until the circles multiply exponentially and explode into infinity.

He was so excited about this process because these circles represented people, and you'd be paid a 5 percent commission on each person (circle) that enters into your business and develops a business of their own, just like you. Obviously, many of you know that this was an opportunity in network marketing, but at the time, I hadn't heard anything about the network marketing industry. I thought I was embarking on a grand and new business adventure.

In network marketing today, the premise is that everyone involved recruits more people in order to sell them the concept of becoming wholesale users who sell to other wholesale users. Basically, this creates a network of wholesale business sellers. Unfortunately, I was unaware that the best network marketing companies to work with are ones with a product line that either is consumable or can generate a residual service, thus making your income the same. Nothing spectacular resulted from my first shot in this industry because of the reason I just mentioned. My lack of emotional motivation, inspiration, and passion were a few other reasons as well. Regardless of my less-than-stellar results in the beginning, I still loved the concept of this wonderful industry and couldn't believe the whole world wasn't involved.

The CD That Inspired My Passion

ONE DAY, I stumbled across a CD that talked about colon cleansing, parasites, intestinal toxins, and all the damage that stems from bowel disorders caused by these toxins. A friend of mine had the CD in his car. I'm not sure if he planted it in front of me on purpose, or if it was just me being nosy, but I saw it and asked about it. He said, "Oh, you should check it out, it talks about bowel stuff, parasites and all the illnesses that people are having because of them." Then he added, "But don't listen to it while you're eating, because it's kind of gross. I promised it to my mom, but you take it and I'll grab it from you on Friday. I have to pass by your neighbourhood anyway."

Brilliant! He took away the pressure and added curiosity, but I was extremely comfortable with him following up with me on Friday. I didn't feel like I was being pitched, hunted down, preyed upon, or cornered into an opportunity. This was just sharing information. I was given this CD without any pressure. Had someone nagged me to listen to it, I probably would have tossed in the back seat of my car and forgotten all about it. This is an extremely valuable lesson for anyone interested in network marketing. Curiosity is a valuable tool!

After listening to the CD, I couldn't believe what I'd heard. You know when something totally takes you by shock? That was me! All my life, I'd suffered from bowel issues, had seen countless doctors and specialists, and had spent many hours in emergency rooms seemingly to no avail. I'm not telling you this because I want to share my medical history with you, but rather to have you understand the one essential element in business — passion. That passion leads you to automatic success.

All of a sudden I had to know: What company produced this CD? Was there a business opportunity? What type of opportunity was it? I loved this CD — it was well done and informative — and I was consumed with the thought of getting more information. So I called my friend and found out that the CD contained information about herbal cleansing products that were sold through a network marketing company. Again, I was so excited having already had some experience in this industry and thought that this could be something big. So, I invited MYSELF to the meeting! How about that one? Another networker's dream. Even better, not only did I just find a product that I was passionate about, but I also remembered a leader from my last network trainings and seminars who inspired me and earned my respect. He taught the concept of "ignorance on fire." What I took from this was to just get on fire and continue doing what works well.

So, on the phone I got, and I told everyone I could think of the layman scoop of this cleansing kit thing that cleans out your colon from parasites and other stuff they wouldn't want to know about. I was simply relaying the information I'd heard from this CD that I was sure was talking right to me, seeing as I had lived through many of the issues on the CD, which included migraines, mood swings, low sex drive, joint pain, fatigue, heartburn, and more. I had so much fun on the phone with my friends that I didn't even realize that they, too, were getting all excited and curious about this wonderful product. This excitement alone stirred so many of them that I had the number one attendance at the meeting, and I wasn't even in business yet.

I attended the meeting, enrolled in the business, and ordered the products immediately, and, in turn, my friends followed suit. Now, in network marketing they often use two terms, and one of them is "up line." These are the people sponsored before you in your line of sponsorship for you to follow; they are somewhat your leaders, depending on the role they decide to take. The other term, of course, is "down line." These are all the people who come into your network after you, whom you are to lead and help build their teams. I always referred to my "down line" members as my partners, only because it had a nicer flare to it.

The Upside of Positivity

I SOON BECAME aware of yet another valuable lesson: Your partners will do what you do, so duplication is another vital element to ensure success. Beware, however, because duplication can just as easily be as negative as it is positive, depending on your actions. If I talk negatively about my "up line," so will my partners. If I dress professionally, so will my partners. If I think and act as though I need to know everything before getting started, so will my partners. If I act excited and inspired using my "ignorance on fire" approach, so will they. It's amazing what people will duplicate, and I learned ever so quickly that negativity spreads even faster than positive action. I guess that's because people always seem to find a loophole to have an excuse not to do things.

At my first meeting, it was as if I was a celebrity. I exuded excitement and showed the enthusiasm to go with it. My next step was to try the products and get everyone else to do the same. So now, here we were, still brand new, just trying the products, and they were working just great, so this added to our belief and kept the enthusiasm going. All of a sudden, positive results started to happen, and "ignorance on fire" was spreading rapidly.

Two people were telling two people, who told two more, and so on. There was no time for negativity, and those who seemed to be negative didn't bother me because I was so busy with the new and excited partners. The ones not interested didn't seem negative to me at all. I didn't have time to play the "convincing" game by calling them over and over, which for sure would have turned them off anyway. I just looked at it as though it wasn't for them at this time but always left them with a positive note or a funny quip just to keep the door open. It's amazing when you get excited about something and you let that excitement shine, you can let everyone decide in their own time what they want to do. Another lesson learned. You know you have a great product; if others can't see it, then it's their loss. Move on.

All of a sudden I was making money, and so were my partners. None of us really had time to study the compensation plan because we were too busy working with wild enthusiasm. When people got in and asked how the money worked, we simply said, "Use your excitement and passion, and visualize the cheques with your name on them. When the money comes, you'll soon figure out how it all works." Now, some of the people in my network insisted on learning the technical stuff, so I led them to those who were technically oriented. No big deal. I wanted to remain the way I was because it was fun and it was working. Why fix what ain't broke?

Eventually I learned about the herbs and the networking aspect because I was so involved in the business and attended every meeting and function. I never let my knowledge show too much because, again, that wasn't duplicable. In time, I realized that within my organization there were herbal experts, compensation plan experts, procrastination experts, "poor me" experts, "know-it-all" experts, and so on. But did I let that bother me? Absolutely not. I was so busy creating "fire," I didn't have time to try to change those people, let alone play convincing games.

As a matter of fact, they loved being who they were, and were, for the most part, happy with their roles. Now, did they ever make the money I did? No, but they were happy with what they had. Did I worry? No, because I still made a residual income off what they sold, so I was happy and they were happy. Would I have made money off their business if I forced them to do what I did? No, because they would've gotten upset and left the business. All I was able to do was guide them through the process using the knowledge and skills that I knew worked the best, and if they wanted to reinvent the wheel, so be it. For those who didn't follow in my footsteps or who left the business, I remained friendly and told them if they found a new system that worked as well as the proven one to let me know. In the end, they were happy to make the money they did, even if it wasn't the top money available to them.

The business world is filled with many different types of people, which is great. Variety is the spice of life, right? Some people want to make a little business out of a big opportunity and are happy doing so. Let them. After all, if you have a happy team, they will always lead you to more. I never wanted to make my business dream become anyone else's. It was important, however, for me to be interested in their dreams. Once I knew what they were, I was able to work with them to accomplish just that. I love knowing other people's dreams and inspiring them to live those dreams no matter what they are. Within each of us is a beautiful dream, and we'd be blessed to find another person who believes in us and who can light that flame inside us to bring birth to that dream. I learned in my networking that this is what life is all about; and what a wonderful way to show it. In the network marketing industry, you become successful only by helping others to become successful. It truly is a wonderful industry.

I couldn't believe what kept happening to me just from enthusiasm alone. Suddenly I was travelling and presenting seminars and qualifying for trips, and had partners in Canada, the United States, Hong Kong, Singapore, Japan, Hawaii, and more. I earned the title "big leader" all because I got caught up in a moment of enthusiasm. As a matter of fact, I was even called the "ignorance on fire" queen.

Today I've extended my dream to share the beauty that lives in the human spirit, which is full of life and enthusiasm, and to help that spirit not only to succeed in business but also to bring it home to our children. No longer am I in network marketing full-time, but my mission remains alive as

I bring a personal spark to children and families, not only through seminars and workshops but also into the homes of the world where the spirit is young and ripe for the journey to begin. Let's give children the dream and put the fire in them to become what we wished for in ourselves. Together we can create real change in this world of chaos, and we can ignite once again the flames of "ignorance on fire."

About Valerie Dee

As an advanced EFT therapist and coach educator, Valerie Dee specializes in mentoring individuals and groups of people to overcome their blocked emotional energy and find their inner rapture. Her expertise lies in inspiring others to become who they really are inside.

Her fifteen years of experience have proven to be a solid reputational foundation as an honest leader within the network marketing industry, with integrity and vision. She teaches that mixed with integrity, if the inner voices and visions become more profound, louder and clearer than any opinions on the outside, you shall be free. Her mission is to bring inspiration and personal spark to relationships and family life not only in seminars and workshops but also in the homes of the world.

Through her coaching practice and workshops, she enjoys success at the Coach Haven.

Together, we create personal change.

Please visit Valerie at
www.deecoachhaven.com

Chapter XVII

SUITED FOR SUCCESS

BY MARLENE MARCO

Chapter XVII

SUITED FOR SUCCESS
by Marlene Marco

Consider this: You have to make a choice. There are two gifts sitting on the table. One is beautifully wrapped in foil paper, topped with a wonderful gold bow and an abundance of trailing ribbons. The other is in a brown paper bag with the top scrunched together and wrinkled just enough so that you can't see inside. You're not allowed to shake, rattle, or peek, and must make the decision in seven seconds based solely on the appearance of the package. Be honest, which gift would you choose?

Now, consider that your potential clients may be overlooking your hidden "gifts" in that first seven seconds, too. Are you willing to take that chance? ***What if...you could give yourself an edge in your business by making a few simple changes?*** Would you agree that creating professional credibility is critical to your bottom line? Think now of a businesswoman that you admire. How would you describe her appearance, attitude, and lifestyle? How does she dress? What makes her stand out in your mind? How does she relate to you and others? Do you enjoy her company? Reflect for a moment on all of her qualities. What is it about her that most stands out in your mind? There's a good chance it's her attractive, professional appearance — her "wrapping" that makes you believe there's something valuable "inside."

In this chapter, the information I'm going to share with you is the result of many years of experience in the business of fashion, direct sales, networking, and people. The common thread, which makes me a student of image, is that most of my businesses have been centred on women. I've watched women who open doors to new and wonderful experiences as well as women, usually unknowingly, who close doors and live in struggle. There are changes all of us can make to create the end result that screams **success!** I've lived many of these changes personally, and it is my desire to mentor other women to be the best that they can be!

How Do Others See You?

IMAGE IS A COMPLETE package. So, let's begin with the most obvious and perhaps the most impactful element — the outer, physical image. What we wear sends a message. What messages are you sending? Are you certain it is the message you want others to hear? Are you demonstrating to the world that you care about yourself? The natural extension of that thought is this: If you care about yourself, you will also care about your clients, your co-workers, and virtually everyone you come in contact with.

One guarantee that comes with image coaching: There will always be a nerve or two that gets touched, and, therefore, someone will almost certainly take offence to something I pass along. That is perfectly okay, because this is designed for your consideration and to give you awareness about the messages you send. If it gives you an edge, then perhaps it is worth considering making a few changes. Life is about making choices. Continue doing what you are doing, and you'll continue getting what you are getting. Making changes will result in changes. Image impacts income.

So that being said, let's get started! Have you analyzed your body type and learned how to dress for the most impact in your business? You've heard it before — there is no way around it. Stand naked in front of a full-length mirror and really see the woman that you are today (not the one you'd like to be). Take some basic measurements. Where do you carry the most weight? Are your hips the wider part of your body, or are your shoulders and chest area? Don't forget to take note of your best features — beautiful eyes, heart-shaped face, great legs, or a wonderful bosom. Now you're ready to work with that beautiful woman. Some basic rules include:

- Dress for who you are, not who you were or who you'd like to be "after you lose a few pounds"! Age-appropriate dress is always respected. Hair bows and frilly skirts are great for teens and twenty-somethings, but they are not appropriate for professional women.
- Dress for your figure type — flaws and all. If you can't change it, learn to work with it. Maximize your assets and minimize your (perceived) liabilities! There are clothes manufactured today for every size and body type. Don't shop in the junior department or buy petites because you wore them in high school or college. You are a grown, professional woman now, and that's the career image you want to portray.

- Figure enhancement is all about illusion and balance. The art of illusion can easily be accomplished by style and colour lines. Dark colours minimize and lighter colours emphasize. Realize the slimming value of vertical lines versus horizontal ones. Simply keep in mind the areas of your body that you'd like to have noticed the most, and use colour, embellishment, and volume on those areas. Trying to keep the attention off certain areas? Darker colours, plainer textures, and a smoother fit will help you achieve that objective.

- Always end a hemline at the narrowest part of a curve on your leg. Similarly, a jacket should end just above or just below the widest part of the hip. You'll avoid the illusion of added width.

- Accessories should be chosen with care. A general rule is that these should be congruent with the size of the wearer, and again, be careful to accentuate the positives. Always try on accessories in front of a full-length mirror — even if it is just a pair of earrings or a purse. It is the complete package that you need to look at. Where does the purse fall beside your body? Does the scarf elongate the look or simply add bulk?

- Professionally styled makeup worn on a consistent basis is important. Keep it basic if that's your look; keep it current if you are a makeup fanatic. Do not wear evening makeup during the day, and when applying your makeup, think about where you're going to be (indoors or outdoors) and apply accordingly. Have you had compliments on your hair in the last week or two? If not, it's time for an update — a colour, style, or suitable cut. Hairstyle, probably more than any other single factor, is always noticed.

If you haven't paid a lot of attention to these details in the past, you may see them as being very superficial, and, arguably, you would be right! However, it is what it is, and it just IS this way — you must create that first impression as one of a polished professional. Dress up, dress down, match, don't match. Fashion trends come and go; rules relax and then tighten up. Here's what I know to be consistent with professional dress for women:

When in doubt, it's always to your advantage to be "overdressed" rather than "underdressed." Dress to be noticed and to be remembered, but not to be shocking or outlandish. Suits with skirts and tailored dresses are a step above. Never underestimate the power of a jacket — you've even heard the term "power suit"! They're not just for men. Classic matching is always more professional. A "power suit" may be costly but is well worth the investment. Even shopping on a budget should include one or two three-piece suits — jacket, skirt, and pants — in a neutral fabric. Classic styling and immaculate fit (often, they will need tailored alterations to achieve this) are well worth the cost. These will take you to any business situation with confidence. If you choose wisely and avoid trends, top-quality clothing items will last for years, making them good investments in your career.

These will be the kind of suits you will put on and forget because you know you look good. You have more important things to think about than whether or not your hem is even, your buttons gape, or your butt looks too big. Gone will be the days of worrying if you look okay — you will know going out the door that you look like the million-dollar deal you are going to close that day! Add in classic shoes — probably pumps, polished to match your look — and you are *fabulous!* Now you can focus on the client, the presentation, or whatever it is that needs to be done well!

How Do You See Yourself?

PROJECTING THE IMAGE of a confident business woman that is polished and refined yet approachable and authentic serves you well in business. Where does the confidence come from? Yes, it comes from knowing you look amazing, but it also stems from the knowledge and attitudes you've developed within. You are the sum total of where you've been and who has influenced you in your life.

What about the influences in our lives? Yes, some are positive, and others are less than ideal. Which ones did you absorb? Here's the question: Do people generally like to be around you? Are you a "people magnet"? If that doesn't describe you, you need to take a long hard look at what's happening within. There is a universal law known as the law of attraction that states that like attracts like. People often use the term "vibrations" when referring to this law. You see, we all send vibrations (energy waves) out into the universe. Our thoughts and actions are vibrations. This law is just as real as the law of gravity. What goes up must come down, and you attract the image you project into the universe. So what are you sending out to those around you? This law is very strong and should be taken seriously.

Send out vibes of strength, belief, and gratitude, and you will find those around you will match those vibrations. Be clear on your intent. Take pride in the business you are building and in the success that you are enjoying! Your presence as you walk into a room will reflect that pride.

All these finishing touches accomplish two important items. Yes, it's all about how others see you. It's also about how you see yourself. You know when you have on an impeccable outfit for the occasion, the perfect fit and the perfect colour, topped off with accessories to die for, you walk taller, you strut — you project confidence that will boost you to the top!

One of my greatest joys in my years of working with women has been to watch timid, uncertain new business owners grow and develop their skills over time. Personal growth is an amazing by-product of networking and direct sales. I know this to be true. I am living proof. For example, at the beginning of my career, public speaking terrified me. I have been very fortunate to have had some amazing mentors over the years, and, through practice, I have fortunately overcome that fear. My confidence and self-esteem have risen to a level that I could previously only have dreamed of. Your confidence can rise too, particularly if you take the time and make the effort to wrap your amazing package so that you intrigue and inspire others.

The System

THE DIRECT SALES industry is the premier environment for growth. There is already a system in place, and by simply plugging in to that system, even when it feels uncomfortable, you will grow and succeed. My twenty-five-plus years in the industry, most of that time in fashion, has been a wonderful time in my life. I've learned that within the safety of that system, I could perform well, succeed, and concentrate on building my business. I no longer needed to concentrate on creating the model. If someone else had done the job before me, I knew that I could duplicate that and equal or surpass that success level.

The level of recognition received in most direct sales businesses is one of the keys to the success in this industry. All of us love a pat on the back and an "Attagirl!" and a few diamond rings and cruises are great too! Kudos and awards are tremendous boosts to our egos and our self-esteem. We create entire teams to cheerlead one another. It's a system that has been proven time and time again to create wealth for both women and men, unheard of in most traditional industries or business environments. I am eternally grateful for the doors that have opened for me through direct sales and, more recently, through networking.

You see, in direct sales, networking is built in. I was networking within my career long before I knew that the *business* of networking even existed. In direct sales, a "hostess" would introduce you to her warm market, and they, in turn, had the opportunity to introduce you to their warm market, and so forth. As a smart professional, you would build relationships and create loyal clients in those new circles. In the *business* of networking, you have increased opportunities to build relationships and ultimately to promote your own business through that developed trust. It was a different mindset for me. I was used to presenting and closing the sale on the spot. Networking isn't like that. It's about building other peoples' businesses. It's about nurturing their passion over and above your own. It's about becoming the "go-to" person. Make yourself into "information central" to both your fellow members and those outside of the organization. Recommend, refer, and win the respect of others, and it will come back to you time and time again.

In 2005, I accepted the position of chapter director with POWE and realized this was a new level of networking. It is a new level of building relationships and connecting people every day. Again, in this safe environment, you can mentor and be mentored, give and receive critical support, and network your way to the top! Regular meetings create a supportive learning environment for the members. Within this organization, we help to build women, enable them to develop their own skill sets, and create their own destinies. In POWE, we take great pride in participating in women's personal development. This leads to self-motivation, which is essential to their success.

Partnering with the POWE founders, Tina and Lia, in 2007 has given me new opportunities to mentor the leadership team in the POWE organization — the chapter directors. As national executive director of training and development, I promote the successful duplication of the system that has evolved over the years of the organization. This allows each director the opportunity to focus on the growth of her chapter area rather than having to reinvent the wheel and create her own system. It's a simple and effective process that is enhanced by the personalities and professional qualities of the chosen leaders.

And, yes, the bottom line is this: We create business. We are capable businesswomen who can be self-supporting or major contributors to the family income. Life is about choices. I, like most of my peers, enjoy a lifestyle of abundance. We've learned to work smart, share our resources, and support one another, and that consistent effort creates better results than procrastination. Keeping our eye on the goal is the only way to get there.

We will do what it takes…and then some.

About Marlene Marco

MARLENE MARCO has built her career in network marketing. She has over twenty-five years' of experience as an award-winning fashion consultant in the Durham region. In her position as senior sales manager, she trained, mentored, and motivated dozens of women to success. She understands the value of creating loyalty and building relationships with her clientele.

In January of 2006, it was a natural move for Marlene to accept the position of Durham West chapter director with the Power of Women Exchange. From there, she partnered with the founders of the association as executive director of training and development. "Creating opportunities for business and professional women to connect and build their businesses is very rewarding."

On a personal note, Marlene loves to spend time with her family. Her son, Zack, daughter-in-law, Tami, and grandchildren, Brad and his little sister Elise, live just minutes away. Marlene considers herself blessed to have healthy energy, a loving and supportive partner, an amazing circle of friends, and abundant possibilities in her life.

Please visit Marlene at
www.powe.ca

Chapter XVIII

MAD ABOUT TECHNOLOGY

BY AZURE CAMPBELL

MAD ABOUT TECHNOLOGY
by Azure Campbell

Once women realize the true power of networking, we can then create an infinite amount of connections by utilizing the associations formed throughout our lives and careers. These relationships are based on time and experience, and, as organized business professionals, we can easily utilize various technologies to assist us in the daily pursuit of both new and existing clients. As many of us know, connections equal business for the self-employed. Whether your database contains a handful of loyal clients or thousands of faceless online purchasers, your ability to track your interactions, such as sales, feedback, or referral business is available to you with a click of your mouse. Many women struggle to integrate the simplest technology into their daily lives; for example, programming the DVR or maximizing the technology in their cars. Some of the technological challenges networkers are facing include:

- New technology "gets in the way" of building a real relationship, which is the key to effective networking.
- Face-to-face interaction is being replaced by online correspondence (email), texting, and social networking on Internet sites.

The benefits of technology available to assist women in growing their businesses are countless. The key, however, is that they must take the first step toward harnessing the power of technology. Are you taking advantage of this basic system of support? It's a lot easier than you might think, and I encourage you not to be intimidated. Women entrepreneurs at all levels of business, from micro to macro-enterprises, should seek to fast-track their skills development to enable them to embrace appropriate technologies. Acquiring a mentor, tech support, and training will help even the most novice of users understand how to leverage technology to work for them, not against them. Yes, even you.

Essential Tools for the Tech-Savvy Gal

TECHNOLOGY SUCH AS computers, scanners, printers, photocopiers, digital cameras, ADSL or broadband, faxes, wireless devices, and VoIP are now priced so that the home-based business operator can afford them. Listed below are some essential tools, which I consider to be "must-haves":

- Computer or laptop – that is the question. The choice is largely personal.
- Personal data devices, like BlackBerry, cell phones, and PDAs. Staying connected is imperative; this gizmo should match your communications style.
- Virtual office – simple steps that prepare your business to go online.
- Storage – external or online backups (databases, email, photos, etc.)
- Web-based email, personal domains — inexpensive solutions are self-serve online.
- Personal security — protect yourself against viruses, pop-ups, and spam. They're everywhere!
- Wireless and wired networks within your home or office — simple, inexpensive solutions can streamline or eliminate the tangle of wires and cords.
- Tax-reporting software or hire a good bookkeeper.
- Video capture — meet face-to-face online via videophones, webcams, or video email, and consider using multimedia on your website. Huge relationship-building potential!
- Small business CRM software — I left the most important for last.

Don't Leave Home Without It

WIKIPEDIA EXPLAINS THAT customer relationship management (CRM) consists of the processes a company uses to track and organize its current and prospective customers. Sounds great, but there is so much more to this often overlooked secret weapon of any successful entrepreneur. Well-designed CRM software is used to support these processes: Information about customers and customer interactions can be entered, stored, and accessed. Typical CRM goals are to improve services provided to clients and to use customer contact information for targeted marketing. Technology change brings entirely new opportunities when automating processes such as invoicing, reminders, and follow-up correspondence.

You will reap incredible benefits from diligently maintaining an accurate account of your business. The time spent will repay you tenfold, just as long as you remember the golden rule: Back up your data! It's up to you how you'd like to use the information you gather about your clients. Do you want to track your referrals? Are you able to report on event profitability? Do you automatically send a quick birthday email to every one of your clients? Does your system of maintaining sales data help you achieve financial goals? Frankly, I'M IN BUSINESS TO MAKE MONEY, and if I'm in the dark about my financial position and am not intimate with my profits and losses, I may as well return to the world of employment. Shudder…

Over the past four years, I've learned that some things make me money and some things don't. So it benefits me to do more of the things that make money. It's a brilliant plan. Spend time on the activities that contribute to your growth, and get control of the details. I urge you to stop contemplating all the "stuff" you should be doing in your businesses. Dig in and get it done. There are many solutions available to you, so it can be intimidating navigating the sea of choice. If necessary, get the assistance you need in this area.

CRM software is the perfect tool to ensure that your clients' needs are being met. It is also the money-making machine that can drive your business if used intelligently. Set yourself apart from the rest, and use technology to your advantage. When I communicate with clients from my home office, order, service history, and invoicing are at my fingertips. I synchronize my contact management software with my wireless cell/data device and take my entire database on the road. I can do my courtesy calls during my travels and sync again upon my return to upload new appointments or order information.

With the power of information in my hands, I'm now able to create automated email campaigns that keep me top of mind. Reminder and calendar functions allow me to make the most of my appointments. Detailed notes are stored for future reference, and expenses and income are tracked. On a regular basis, I refer to profit/loss reporting on events, shows, and/or demos, and I track viral marketing efforts and referral business when wondering where to spend my promotional dollars. Today's economy is shying away from big box stores, and no one likes being treated like a number. Intelligent use of contact and client information can produce business where you thought there was none. Use this power carefully, and pay attention to consumer rights and the current privacy policies that are in place. Encourage your clients to specify their preferred communication styles, and honour their preferences. Don't fret when someone opts out of your newsletter campaign. It's nothing personal.

The Dark Side of the World Wide Web

THOSE OF US who love to network realize that the Internet has the potential to greatly enhance our networking experiences. However, for some, the Web casts a great divide among our social networks; many find this age of texting, emailing, and online videos alienating and lacking the personal touch. Our activity on the Internet can be as little as the odd email to as much as ambitious online marketing initiatives that create a wider exposure. Most will agree that the Web and email are impersonal (and due to the absence of context and the nuances of body language, they often lead to misunderstandings), while others find them utterly convenient and even indispensable. In my opinion, both are right.

Here are some tips that will help you maintain a strong balance:
- True business building is done in person.
- A barrage of uninvited email forwards or business announcements can sour a budding relationship quickly. Once your email address gets relegated to the junk mail folder, it's almost impossible to work your way out.
- Email doesn't replace a phone call.
- Phone calls don't replace an in-person meeting.

Our intuitive understanding is that face-to-face communication is the most persuasive. In reality, of course, it's not always possible to meet in person, so email prevails. How, then, do people react to persuasion attempts via email? Persuasion research has uncovered fascinating effects: Men appear to be more responsive to email because it bypasses their competitive tendencies (Guadagno and Cialdini, 2002). Women, however, may respond better in face-to-face encounters because they are more "relationship-minded." But is this finding just a gender stereotype?

Do you want to profit from email marketing? For the majority of women, the answer is a resounding yes. So I've included five tips to help you.

- **Tip #1: Address Recipients with Their Name in Email Campaigns.** Make your newsletter recipients feel more like themselves and less like mere numbers by greeting them individually and personally. This will show them you didn't just spam out thousands of emails to an anonymous list. Connect with your customers on an individual basis, and your profits will grow.

- **Tip #2: Create a Clear Call to Action in Email Marketing Campaigns.** Make sure recipients of your email marketing message know what you expect them to do and also what they can expect from you. Nothing is more confusing to an email recipient than a message that "beats around the bush"; one way to not profit with email marketing is to confuse your customers or leave them without an explicit "next step."

- **Tip #3: Preview the Deal at the Top.** Move your boring information (product details, disclaimers, etc.) down the email page; lead the email with your "best offer" in colourful graphics or exciting, enticing wording. If the very first part of your email catches your customers' attention, they will read the email and will be more likely to follow up. Pay particular attention to the subject line, which should be so intriguing that the recipient simply must open the message and read it. There are actually marketing copywriters who specialize in headlines/subject lines because they are so critically important.

- **Tip #4: Ease Up on the Exclamation Points and Question Marks.** The path to successful email marketing is not paved with exclamation marks and ampersands. The idea is to bold the important words and bring out others with colours and, sometimes, italics. If you emphasize everything, you are emphasizing nothing. Nothing is more annoying and unprofessional to a prospective customer than seeing this!!!!!!!!!!!! !!!!!!!!!!!!!!!!!!!!!!! So be careful with your overuse of symbols such as "!" and "&".

- **Tip #5: Make Landing Pages Fit Your Email Marketing Campaign.** An email marketing campaign is worth nothing without a landing page, so make sure it visually belongs to its campaign and does not irritate the user. The style, type, and colours should fit closely to the landing page of your campaign. Another way to help avoid confusion is to make sure these two look very closely related and are designed as if they are one cohesive campaign.

Here are some ways that I've built a network that grows exponentially by effectively using key tech tools and a constantly evolving online presence:

Set Targets

AS NETWORKING EVENTS are often more social in nature than prearranged meetings, you need to set targets and goals to make sure your time is used effectively. You are better off making real connections with less people than you are making casual connections with many people. It is the quality versus quantity paradigm, and in this instance, quality wins. Try meeting four new people and catching up with four old connections. Having a specific target for the event keeps you focused and prevents wasting valuable marketing time.

Maximize every unexpected meeting and every unplanned encounter. Every social event, every outing, and every encounter is an opportunity to network, so remember to use these occasions to hand someone your card. You never know when you might meet someone who can help you or who knows someone else who could. While the information is still fresh, record any details that may come in handy during future correspondence.

Follow Up

THERE IS NO point in making connections with people if you are not going to follow up and continue to build the relationship. Create a follow-up system that should include a thank you card or note. An email asking their permission to be added to your email list and arranging another face-to-face catch-up are critical to making a true connection, not just collecting another card.

Use "in your face" follow-up. "Out of sight, out of mind" is the operative phrase to remember when you're wondering why no one's calling. Follow-up is the most essential step to take if you see potential from someone who has your card. Keep track of these leads using your contact management software, and be persistent. A business card does not get you the job; it opens the door just enough for you to do the rest.

Use Emails to Yourself as Reminders

USERS SHOULD BE able to create "to-do's" with their email software. There are tricks you can use, such as emailing yourself at a future date. If someone tells you to call back in three months, it is possible to place an email in most systems with a future mail date. Forward yourself the email to arrive in your inbox just before the date in question. This keeps you totally on top of all situations. Some software offers a calendar feature, and a preset reminder will pop up on your computer screen.

Your External Business Face

ONCE YOU PRESENT yourself and your business, you have to make sure you can back up your image with a professional external identity; i.e., logo, website, business cards, thank you cards, stationery, marketing collateral, and so forth.

Blog It

NOWADAYS, IF YOU haven't started a blog (weblog, or online journal), you are missing out on some of the best free marketing that exists, leading readers to your website or landing page for no money. Not blogging causes you to lose out on countless contacts and potential customers. It's a fact. Warm-blooded humans love to read blogs. Search engines such as Google and Yahoo! adore blogs. For the search engines, the reason is fairly simple: Content is constantly updating, and search engines feed off these updates (it's called "crawling"). Much of the best in information, resources, and product reviews (as well as products themselves) can be gleaned from following good blogs. It's easy to create reader and customer loyalty and keep your readers coming back for more when you have your own space to pour your heart and soul into.

The key to successfully starting your own blog is to first know your limitations. You must have the know-how to make your blog stand out from all the hundreds of thousands (if not millions) of other bloggers. If you do not know how to draw traffic to your blog, you face the same trials and tribulations as you would setting up a static website. You must know how to increase traffic, draw and keep visitors, and use the tools and tricks of blogging to be successful. But none of that is difficult to do; setting up a blog can be done in as little as five minutes.

Let's presume, for now, that you are only interested in the first stepping stones to creating a successful blog. Your first step would be to determine your passion. Bloggers who are passionate about their fields, hobbies, businesses, politics, and so on joyfully exchange information regularly with their readers. Conversely, individuals who choose to blog about subjects in which they have no real know-how, passion, or expertise tend to quickly abandon their projects. As the saying goes, no heart, no blog.

It's as Easy as 1, 2, 3

THIS IS A basic format to help you begin. Once you start this process and identify the right strategic connections, you'll have a clear path to those with whom you can create profitable relationships. Be confident, be clear, and be concise! And remember to keep doing things that make you money.

So, now that you've seen the benefits of technology, instead of surrendering to it, it's time we take control and harness its power. Agree to invest the time and set aside a budget to learn how to thrive with technology and to maximize its usefulness in your life and business. To do that, there are three simple maxims to consider:

1. Technology is simpler than it looks.
2. Humans are behind all technology.
3. All technology is interconnected.

Once we realize and understand these principles, we are able to put technology in the proper context, determine which technology is right for our business, and use it to maximize our productivity. With time, we will all be well on our way to reducing the amount of technology-related stress in our lives. Have confidence that you, too, can control the beast.

About
Azure
Campbell

AZURE CAMPBELL has over ten years' experience in end-user training, migration consulting, project management, courseware development, requirements analysis, business analysis, and leadership. In addition to her extensive career in the IT field, she is also an accomplished public speaker. Some of the groups she has spoken to include the Payne Group, various chapters of PMI (Project Management Institute), Future Shop, Direct Selling Women's Alliance, and the Seven Sisters law firms. She has also presented numerous workshops, seminars, and training classes since 1998 to approximately five thousand participants on three different continents.

Azure has an established reputation as a national leader in technology education, with a strong record of technical workforce development through quality training and certification programs. As a qualified computer trainer, Azure's mission is to provide personalized computer training in a relaxed, stress-free environment. She specializes in helping small business owners, busy executives, and individuals to establish their telecom needs and to learn the skills required to achieve their technology goals through training, support, and mentorship.

Learn more about Azure at
www.absolutelyright.acnnrep.com, or contact her at
absolutelyright@acnrep.com

Chapter XIX

IT'S MORE THAN JUST A SIGN
ON THE LAWN; IT'S CALLED
"MAKING FRIENDS"
BY TRACY DONNELLY

Chapter XIX

IT'S MORE THAN JUST A SIGN ON THE LAWN;
IT'S CALLED "MAKING FRIENDS"
by Tracy Donnelly

"Hi! My name is Tracy. Do you have anyone I can play with?" This familiar chant was heard throughout the neighbourhood whenever someone new moved in. I was four, and my family lived in the second occupied house in a brand new subdivision, so every time I saw a moving truck rumbling by, it made me very happy. Off I'd run to see who was moving in and to joyfully welcome them to the neighbourhood! I didn't know it then of course, but that was the start of my networking career.

When September arrived, it was time for me and the other kids who had moved into the neighbourhood to go to the "new" school. It was nerve-wracking and exciting at the same time. I believe the title of Robert Fulghum's book All I Really Need to Know I Learned in Kindergarten is true. At least it was for me. Our teacher, Mrs. Wade, somehow made it possible for all of us to feel welcome, be comfortable, and learn how to communicate with each other. She arranged for us to sit across from each other on the carpet and had us ask questions about each other — about our brothers, sisters, and pets, and what we wanted to be when we grew up. She then introduced us to the other classes and invited the teachers inside, and we learned a bit about the other classes too. Each of us new arrivals, teachers and students alike, started with this common ground of basic information about each other, which enabled us to form groups and friendships based on similar backgrounds. Who knew that all I needed for a real estate career, I'd learn in kindergarten? But I did.

Every meeting with each client today consists of the same basic questions. Interesting, isn't it, how common questions give you a bit of insight into how similar and yet how different we all are. They communicate and connect with me based on the answers to those questions. From their

184

expressed dreams and desires, I can then relate based upon my own similar experiences and the experiences I've heard from other clients. This process feeds into the databank that is my mind. A nice aspect about the relationship business is that no matter where you are, the basic premise is the same. Where do you want to go? What do you love about this house? What don't you love and what is on your wish list or need list for the next home? Regardless of the specific answers, the result is always the same: It's time for a change.

Making the Rounds

MANY TIMES THROUGHOUT my life, Dad would come home from work and announce over dinner that we were moving. The first couple of times were heart-wrenching. My friends, my room, my stuff! Once, it was November 1st and my greatest concern was my Halloween bucket. I was sure the movers had been into it! As the years progressed, it became easier, or at least a little more acceptable and manageable. As a matter of fact, I made it into a system where I'd make the goodbye rounds. Part of those last conversations included asking if they had any relatives or friends in the new city. We would even ask our butcher and dry cleaner and hairdressers if they knew where to get the best meat, cleaning, or haircuts in our next city. This system became a trusted lifeline and enabled us to have an instant "inside contact" in our new hometown.

When you have established, even for a short time, a relationship based upon service and trust, unknowingly, you want to find that comfort zone in your new city. It may not be formal networking as we know it in the corporate world, but for the corporation of running a household, it is the way the world runs. There's something to be said for those women in the park with their youngsters, chatting away on benches, exchanging notes or recipes. Or those coffee klatches that used to occur, swapping valuable information, but minus the gossip of course! The men would do their networking with discussions over the lawn mower or standing beside the BBQ grill. If you needed to know something or wanted to know where to get the best whatever, that was the source.

Every time we moved to cities armed with that valuable information in hand, whether it was to look up a store or a relative of someone from our old city when we got there, we needed to join and get out there as soon as possible to create a new sense of belonging. One time, a store clerk assured us that he would call ahead to his cousin in our new town and make sure we were looked after. It was always a great upheaval for all, and understanding how difficult it is for some people to change postal codes let alone cities comes from deep within me. Part of the residual effects of moving enabled me to resolve to create a system for people to make contact with the basics in each new city. The concept of "welcome wagon" helped greatly, and yet it can go much deeper. When given the opportunity, the value of receiving an introduction to neighbourhood services and what the city has to offer is immeasurable.

Looking back now, one of the last moves my family and I made was a particularly difficult one, and yet it also seemed easy. The ease came from our realtor, who did go above and beyond to make sure our family was settled and taken care of in our new town. Her sister lived in our new destination. She made a personal visit to us, and from then on, we became fast friends. She introduced our family to her friends, invited us to social events, and ensured that schools, banking, and shopping concerns were all met. It was similar to having your own personal concierge while the boxes were being unpacked. She even went so far as to make sure my brother and I had peers our age at some gatherings, and helped to expand our social circles. I recall thinking at the time that this was how it should always be. She wasn't even in real estate, yet she understood the importance of people connecting to people, and even if the only thing in common was a new face in the group, at least after the weather and traffic is discussed you can find a few more things to ask.

These experiences helped me tremendously when I spread my wings and forged out on my own to university — now there's a networking experience if I've ever seen one. An entire community of brand new students thrust upon a campus, all scared and nervous at the same time and yet with a huge mission of finding classrooms and succeeding at studies. Again, it was my personal undertaking to meet and greet as many people as I could and, with the help of the residence advisor, connect with as many friends as possible. The sooner that happens, the sooner everyone becomes comfortable, relaxed, and "safe" and can get on with their business. Ironically, the benefit of networking surfaces when you encounter someone in a new situation whom you've known from another part of your life. Two people who are away from home, separated by moves and different cities, yet you meet in the hallway while moving in. *There's nothing as reassuring as a familiar face in a sea of strangers!*

Put One Foot in Front of the Other

THERE ARE SO many people that become paralyzed with fear when faced with walking into a room full of people they don't know. The key is to hold your head up...don't look down at your feet...they will be okay...just put one foot in front of the other and move on. The first person with whom you make eye contact is the first person you should acknowledge and respond to. Smile and say, "Hi." If the room is full, comment on the great turnout; if it's still early, say something along the lines of, "Gee, I guess I'm lucky I got here before everyone else. That gives us a chance to talk." Say anything, but make it positive, to break the ice. That first contact is usually the best one; that person is somehow "tuned in," or connected, to you. I have found this to be true again and again. If you weren't invited by someone who is already there, you can always start with that first person and go from there. Unless you do know someone there, you can always make conversation, even as simple as asking the person what they do, or how they found out about the gathering. Perhaps they are shy or intimidated and your questioning will give them an opportunity to warm up.

At every meeting or event, no matter which kind, there is always someone in the group who fulfills the role of "the connector." This person is the first who comes to mind when you need someone or some service. You snap your fingers and say, "Hey, I know, I'll call [the connector]. He [or she] will know the answer!" Sometimes it's great to be that person, other times, you need to call in backup! Whether it was in my public school life, at university, or in my corporate career days, there was always a connector, and eventually I became that person. One advantage of moving or changing jobs is that you develop your own set of resources, and, by maintaining the relationships already established, each move brings on a new addition to the network web. Before the Internet existed, we were connecting to people around the world by mail and telephone and the ever-popular personal visit.

Each location, however, has its unique set of rules or guidelines of operation, which is quite prevalent in the corporate world. A hierarchy exists, and it is frowned upon for someone to overstep the bounds, especially when making that ever-so-important first impression. The introductions are done in a systematic and organized fashion, and it is bad form to "go up the ladder" too fast or aggressively. You may still get there; just make sure you progress according to the proper steps. Don't skip rungs on the ladder, as you may alienate someone.

These guidelines are also visible in a mixed networking group, if you take time to observe. A hierarchy exists. The sole proprietor or individual business owner also has an interesting perspective. Having my own business, independent of real estate, also opens up a whole world, and occasionally that "lone wolf" position is both rewarding and daunting. You are in a networking situation with no corporate credo to fall back on — or blame. If you're lucky enough to run across someone who genuinely takes an interest in your business, it can be a soul-searching exploration of the whys and wherefores you do what you do.

Take a Genuine Interest

FOR MOST OF us, we've learned that the most productive and results-oriented connection is one in which you actually spend some time getting to know someone. Each of us in our own right has a fascinating life. But like icebergs, in networking or social situations we only scratch the surface. How can you know if a person you meet is the one you need, or who may need you, if you don't take a few minutes to have a genuine two-way conversation with them? It's not about what they can do for you, but what you can do for them. There's an old real estate adage, a favourite saying of one of my mentors, Floyd Wickman: "People don't care what you know until they know that you care."

It is important to bear in mind that you never know who or where new business will be generated. More important, every action and conversation you have can make or break your business. If you are genuinely and sincerely interested in people and care about them, then you will reap tenfold. The law of attraction states that like attracts like, and this plays a large part in networking and every aspect of life. Each business and person has a delicate balance of emotion and logic.

Following the concept of "going three-deep" is also an important aspect of the Keller Williams philosophy. Strangely, it's something I was already doing before I knew its origins or its name. It is the method of asking questions and actually going into three layers, similar to peeling an onion, to find out the deeper meaning to the often surface-only answers to the questions. This process can work in almost any situation. For example, if someone says they want to move to a larger house, I don't know why they want to do that without asking a series of questions that will get to the bottom of the real reason for the move. It could be because the family is growing, because they are going to be multigenerational, or because they have just outgrown the current residence and want enough space to stretch their legs, so to speak. It is not being nosy to probe for deeper answers; it is trying hard to be the best provider (in my case, real estate professional) one can be.

The underlying reasons for why we do things are not always evident on the surface. As a networker who thrives and survives on building rapport, you develop an actual relationship and cement the relationship further by caring enough to really find out how that new person feels. It's not a matter of rattling off question after question either, like an interrogation. It is important to ask, listen, and comprehend, and from each answer a conversation develops that can drift off on tangents. Each meander can take you closer to the true need and offer the solution of how you can provide them with help and benefits.

Be it residential, investment, or commercial real estate, there is always an emotional side as well as an educated business decision. It is my responsibility to ensure that all options and possibilities are presented to a client for them to make an informed choice. To understand the emotions and also be able to present the cold facts is a delicate balancing act. Admittedly, most of the time it is much easier to be on my side of the table than yours!

It is that understanding and passion that continues to drive me onward to expand my circle and add to it for the benefit of my clients. It is my continuing effort to create networks and groups in my local area, as well as around the world, that can assist anyone moving in or out of those places. I have already established connections in other cities and countries that would benefit anyone to move there or even just to visit. It's a great thing to go on vacation, and, if necessary, have a contact that can assist or lend help. Can you imagine going to a foreign country where they don't speak your language and running into a situation where you need help? Going to the embassy isn't always convenient or accessible, or even necessary. Yet, if you had a personal contact who had been informed that you were going to be there and had an introduction, and, if needed, you could call them, if nothing else, the peace of mind you'd have while you're away would be a benefit.

Pieces of the Puzzle

AS A CHILD, I learned early on about emotional upheaval. Relating to families, talking to the children, allaying their fears, and offering choices and solutions are pieces of the puzzle we're trying to assemble. Every family member, including pets, is a puzzle piece. My passion is completing the border and filling in all the pieces. That includes all components of a network system that sends out ripples, connecting all the pieces to make it a whole.

A friend who had moved many times said recently, "It would have been great to have met you earlier in our moves and at least have the guidance instead of being thrust into a new city all alone!" That's a great compliment that I accept gladly but with humility. It's not a process I undertake on my own. I have a great team! With help, we would like to inspire likeminded people to expand and fill their circles with contacts from all walks of business and community life. It's not every day that you buy or sell a house, but you may know someone who is moving, and — you never know — I just may know someone who needs your expertise. It's all in whom you know who is reliable, consistent, compassionate, and "top of mind!"

About

Tracy

Donnelly

TRACY DONNELLY offers environmental solutions and conservation management in all aspects of real estate. With a Bachelor of Environmental Studies from the University of Waterloo and over twenty years of consulting experience in helping families find homes, investments, commercial property, and relocation information, as well as her own personal experience from multiple personal moves, Tracy is prepared to answer your plea for help and will ease the anxiety surrounding your move.

"We're ready when you are!" is the motto by which Team Donnelly conducts their lives and business. As your "green" realtor, Tracy can also assist you with implementing environmentally conscientious plans and materials for remodelling, preparing to sell, or updating your home. With certificates in appraisals, mortgage financing, real estate law, identity theft, and personal-property legal care and negotiations, among others, Tracy continues to improve her level of services and expertise in order to provide clients with a broad network of support. The decorators, financial advisors, packers/movers, and everyone in between become solutions. Being a wife and mother of four active children, combined with running a full business operation plus being active in volunteer groups and honouring networking commitments, Tracy's busy days lead to contentment and satisfaction.

Please visit Tracy at
www.teamdonnelly.ca

Chapter XX

STARTING OVER

— AND OVER —

AND OVER AGAIN

BY SHIRLEY BANKEY

Chapter XX

STARTING OVER — AND OVER — AND OVER AGAIN
by Shirley Bankey

A s I sat to write this chapter, my first thoughts were, "What do I know? What have I learned? What can I share? Can I inspire and encourage women to step out of their comfort zone?" The answers are: Lots, lots, lots, and yes! You see, I know about starting over — and over — and over again. You can reach your hopes, dreams, and desires, no matter how many times you have to start over. Thirty-six years ago, I married Don, the most marvellous man in the world, and we had two children, Lisa and Erik. We have lived in eleven cities and fifteen homes. My theme song could easily be "On the Road Again" by Willie Nelson.

I have learned how to get up and get going again, real fast. And we learned to take turns compromising. Love may be the first key ingredient to a lasting relationship, but compromise is a close second. Not everyone in a relationship can have everything they want, when they want it, all the time and have everyone still be happy. So a mutual decision was made that Don would pursue his career and I would first stay home with the children until they were in school, and then it would be my turn. I am grateful for the luxury of having had that valuable time with the kids. Today, that is just a dream for most parents.

Having moved so much, I learned how to quickly and efficiently make my new house a warm and loving home. I also learned how to network my way into new surroundings and my new dream career. Networking is a great tool to build both businesses and personal relationships.

- It establishes mutually beneficial relationships.
- It links people we know to people they know.
- It introduces people who share interests and activities.

Most people don't realize they are networking when they move. Think about all the people you meet in the process: real estate agents, movers, school teachers, coaches, bankers, service providers, and your new neighbours. All these people help you and your family integrate into the new area. They are happy to share everything they know about your new town: where to shop, who is the best painter, where to get your car repaired, and so on. Don't wait. Go ring your neighbour's doorbell and introduce yourself. Take the opportunity to meet the other parents as you stand around the ball field, hockey arena, or ballet studio. Speak up and ask for what you need.

- "Do you know a good daycare for my son?"
- "Is there a good hairdresser close by?"
- "I'm new in town. I'm a decorator…know anyone who needs one?"

TRY NOT TO be shy. I've found that shy people are often misperceived as aloof and arrogant. So smile, make eye contact, and go for it. Once you settle into your home, become a good friend and neighbour. Invite neighbours over for coffee and cookies. Don't wait to get all organized and decorated, and don't worry about baking cookies — store-bought is fine. Make the effort to meet new and interesting people. A terrific new friend could be just across the street, at the gym, or standing beside you at the arena.

The whole process of selling your home, house hunting, packing, saying your goodbyes, moving, eating fast food, unpacking, and settling everyone into their new lives can leave you with no energy for yourself. Before you know it, you are plunked on the sofa with a box of chocolates, watching a soap opera, feeling sorry for yourself. Been there, done that, didn't like it, so here is my solution: Start eating healthy and join an exercise class right away. You'll meet new people and get healthier too. Yes, more networking. The perk here is you get to shop for a new exercise outfit first. Now that you are feeling better, get out there and find what you want, what you need for yourself. If you are the engine that runs your family, how are you going to do that if you don't take care of yourself? It's not selfish to tend to your own needs; it's practical.

Because I have moved so many times, I have been able to try many different things. I have been a dressmaker, an artist, a decorator, a commissioned salesperson, and a small business owner, to name just a few. Some roles I loved, and some I did not. Some were successful, and some not so much. Each opportunity was a learning experience about myself, my strengths and weaknesses, my values, and my passions. Each one taught me valuable lessons and increased my knowledge. Each one brought new fears to conquer. I didn't let fear stop me from trying new things. A failure is a failure only if you do not learn from it. I am attending the school of life, and I don't plan on graduating until I leave this earth.

One of my successes was Idle Tyme Crafts, a retail store in Peterborough. It was an arts and crafts supply store, picture-framing studio and art studio/classroom. I sold my car to raise money to open it. (If you want something badly enough, there is usually a way to get it, and the walks I took in the morning and at night were added health benefits.) Through Idle Tyme Crafts, I learned about networking and balancing my family life and career life.

I started in a small store in a hard-to-find location, with one student in my first class and very little money for advertising. Who am I kidding? I had no money for advertising, but I wasted some on it anyway. My real growth came from word of mouth, or, I should say, networking and referrals. That one student plus friends and family spread the word, and within a year, I had broken through the wall to double my space and had a huge classroom and six to eight people per class.

Before I finished cleaning up the plaster dust from my expansion, another opportunity dropped right into my lap. A shop owner carrying a similar line was in shopping and offered me her better location, as she was moving on to something new. Why did I have this great luck? Because I made sure my lines complemented what she offered. I made sure I networked with her so we could help more customers find what they were looking for. I blended the best of what I had to offer with the best of what she had to offer.

I was now in a good location with double the space, double the lines of merchandise. and, of course, double the debt. I grew again and moved to an even larger and better location just a short distance away. This success and growth was, again, the result of networking and referrals. I held my classes around a table where everyone could see each other, get to know each other, and have fun, all while learning something new. I then benefited from referrals when they did "show-and-tells" with their friends and family. I used the classroom to hold business improvement meetings with the surrounding business owners, as well. When you work as a networking team within your community, everyone prospers.

Five exciting years passed, and Don was presented with another great career opportunity. It was time to make more life-altering decisions, compromises, and changes. After weighing all the options and looking at the retail climate, we sold the business and the house and were "On the Road Again." To some, it may seem that I had sacrificed a lot. That I had placed my needs, wants, and desires last. If you knew me, however, you would realize I am no pushover. I am quite capable of standing firm and demanding what I fairly deserve.

Let's talk about compromise again. The perk of being single is you can afford to put yourself first, most of the time. But a lasting and loving relationship takes more consideration. As soon as you add children into the mix, it becomes a challenge to keep everyone happy. Taking turns becomes essential. Women often put everyone else's needs ahead of their own. You deserve equal consideration. Being a wife and mother does not mean you go immediately to the end of the line. You do, sometimes, get to pass "Go."

When it comes to family, career, and personal time, most women feel as if they are walking a tightrope and one false move will send them tumbling without a safety net. You can map out your day planner with precision, but all it takes is an ill child, a flat tire, or a traffic jam, and there goes your cherished personal time. I try to schedule in extra time for such mishaps, and, if all goes well, the extra time is pure luxury.

This brings to mind the age-old question women ask: "Can we have it all?" Yes, absolutely! But, not all at once — not everything at the same time. Spread it out over a lifetime, and the answer will be "Yes, of course, you can have it all." Each stage of life brings to light new priorities, new values, and new passions. Take your time. Enjoy what each stage has to offer, as it rarely presents itself again.

I must admit that I was not always happy with all the changes in my life. I will also admit to a few tears and temper tantrums. Despite my worries and concerns, most changes turned out for the best. Everyone experiences change: promotions, job cuts, downsizing, marriage, divorce, empty-nesting, re-nesting, and retirement — some positive and some negative, depending on your point of view at the time. Make it easier on yourself. Choose to see a change as a fresh new start, with endless and exciting possibilities around every corner.

I am a rare breed. I love networking. It's fun. It doesn't feel like working to me. I do have a moment of nervous stage fright upon entering a room full of strangers, but once I get into the thick of things, I really enjoy myself. I like people, and I like getting to know them and what they do. When one person tells another about your business, and they tell someone else, and so on, you are building a huge network of new referrals that you can leverage to grow your business.

Here is my take on successful networking:

- **TIP #1:** Take the time to really listen. Be genuinely interested in meeting new people and getting to know them. Be authentic and approachable. The quality of your interactions is more important than the quantity. It is not about you only. Networking is a two-way relationship.

- **TIP #2:** Humour, laughter, and a smile are a girl's best friends. Whoever said it was diamonds was greatly mistaken. Use the gifts of humour, laughter, and a smile, and you can afford your own diamonds. Humour should never be sarcastic, hurtful, off-colour, loud, or abrasive.

- **TIP #3:** Patience is a virtue. Networking will not give you instant results. It takes time for people to get to know you, like you, and trust you. Be persistent, and attend the same networking events regularly. It will take six months to a year for the results of your efforts to show.

- **TIP #4:** Cell phone etiquette is vitally important. Do not give a caller more value than you give the interesting person you are with. It's insulting. Cell phones should be turned off during networking events, unless you need to be reachable in an emergency. Even then, if a call comes in that you must take, politely excuse yourself, explain that it's an emergency, and step outside to take the call.

- **TIP #5:** Keep a networking journal. Track which networking events work best for your business. Who is your ideal client? What networking events do they attend? Think outside the box and be on the lookout for new ways to expand your networking circles.

Wonder where my journey has taken me now? Don and I have a beautiful grandson. When I look into Liam's blue eyes, my heart almost bursts with love. What a wonderful gift he is. I am confident that there will be more gifts to come, and I have room in my heart for every one of them. They will keep me young.

I am now an independent associate with Pre-Paid Legal Services, Inc. What a great company, with a service that truly helps many people. I am proud to be a part of it. I cannot imagine ever retiring, as I am having a lot of fun and it gives me a great excuse to keep networking. I can also see a few more moves in my future, but no worries. Pre-Paid Legal can move with me. Before I am done, I think I would like to aim for thirteen cities and seventeen homes. I am grateful for my past and look forward to my future.

You see, your future holds endless possibilities. Believe in yourself. Have courage. Cherish this day-to-day flight through life. It's what makes it all worth living. Take a leap of faith, and soar to success. Enjoy the dips, dives, and butterflies.

About Shirley Bankey

SHIRLEY BANKEY is a wife, mom, grandmother, and business-woman. Her years juggling home life, school plays, hockey tournaments, and several successful businesses were happy. Family was her priority. Owning a business she was passionate about was a bonus.

Her creative interests include gardening, decorating, renovating, and painting watercolours. A natural networking coach, Shirley enjoys building personal and business relationships and is always willing to lend a helping hand. Southern Ontario is home, but her business has the capability to expand throughout North America.

Shirley's successes in small business prepared her for her current business. She is an independent associate with Pre-Paid Legal Services, Inc., a seasoned NYSE-listed company that has revolutionized the legal industry. Pre-Paid Legal membership provides legal council to average people and small businesses anywhere, at any time, night or day, at an affordable cost. With Pre-Paid Legal, Shirley makes a difference through helping others, and she makes a nice living too.

Identity theft is a new criminal enterprise that has become an epidemic. Shirley's workshops teach attendees how to prevent becoming a victim of identity theft. Pre-Paid Legal's Identity Theft Shield is an affordable solution to this growing crime.

Want the best of the best in your corner? Join Pre-Paid Legal. It's peace of mind. *Visit Shirley at www.prepaidlegal.com/hub/shirleybankey, or contact her at shirley@ppl-legal.ca*

Chapter XXI

INSIDE/OUT: CORPORATE TO COURAGEOUS

BY LINDA CATTELAN

Chapter XXI

INSIDE/OUT: CORPORATE TO COURAGEOUS
by Linda Cattelan

For twenty-six years, I was a banker. Three years ago, I left banking and my life changed dramatically. In reality, my transformation began approximately five years before I had the courage to leave the corporate world. Since officially entering the entrepreneurial realm, I've been on a personal journey filled with many exciting changes.

My fundamental belief about life is that everything happens to us as a result of our own doing and being. On some level, either knowingly or unknowingly, we attract our destiny to ourselves. We are a work in process and are constantly evolving as human beings. Life truly is a journey, and throughout this chapter, I will share a few lessons I've learned about myself and networking along the way.

Lesson #1: Build Your Networking Muscles. I didn't think I had any networking muscles until I left banking. Suddenly, I was on my own in the professional coaching field, attempting to build business contacts. I didn't believe I was a good networker, yet many of my colleagues who also took the entrepreneurship road would say to me, "Wow, you know a lot of people."

Many of us have strange misconceptions about what networking is. Many people think of networking as cold calling, or building a Rolodex of potential prospects. I certainly shared that perspective. Some think of networking as a "how-to" process. Networking isn't about the "how"; it is just about building relationships.

Early in my banking career, I opened a neighbourhood branch bank. I made it a point to ensure all the correct steps were taken. Two months before the scheduled opening, I hired the staff and prepared for business. After doing so, I immediately set out to meet every merchant and professional in the community to simply introduce myself and let them know that we would open in the community soon.

I joined the local business development association and regularly attended the meetings. By the time the branch officially opened, I had secured almost seventy merchant accounts and several mortgages, and on opening day, there was a line of customers waiting to open accounts. It was one of the most successful bank branch openings in the history of the company. I still remember the fun the staff and I had in building that branch and its business. I didn't think of it as networking at the time. I thought I was simply introducing myself to the community.

So, where did I develop my networking muscles? In the community. I was, and still am, good at building relationships. Many networking opportunities were available in my corporate career, including talking to customers. Those who valued my service often referred me to their friends, family, or colleagues. Some of them followed me from branch to branch, and some I still see to this day, and they are some of my closest friends. Over time, small talk became deeper conversations, and then close friendships developed, which I still cherish today.

Lesson #2: Develop Thick Skin. You have to have thick skin to be a successful small business owner. People, even your true friends, don't always return your calls promptly or reply to your emails, or read your newsletters or articles. At times, you feel ignored, perhaps even rejected. So a thick skin is essential.

You must continue to tell yourself how great you are, how wonderful your service is, and how much business you're going to get as soon as the word is out. Celebrate every little win. I celebrate every time someone returns my phone call or someone wants more information or someone wants to get together with me for coffee or lunch. You must be willing to step outside the box from time to time. Be courageous and take a chance by doing something you wouldn't normally do. Remember, anything is possible when you believe in yourself.

As a hockey mom, not only do I get to be proud of my kids, but I also get to enjoy the game and socialize with the other parents. Sitting on the sidelines for many years taught me to develop a love, appreciation, and good understanding for the game. After my children's games, I would often say to them, "You played a really good game." Or, "I really liked that one save you made." Or, "I really liked that slapshot." Or, "You weren't skating as fast as you usually do." Or, "You weren't 'on' the way you usually are."

And then my kids would ask, "What do you know about hockey? You've never played the game. If it's so easy, then why don't you do it?"

Taking risks is a great way of developing thick skin. And so it didn't take much ribbing from my kids for me to decide that if they thought I lacked credibility, I would take up the game of hockey. So, at the age of forty-five, with no personal hockey experience and only average skating ability, I joined a women's hockey league to prove to my kids and to myself that I could be more than just a spectator or commentator at a hockey game. I honestly believe you can do anything you set your mind to.

So there I was, as excited and nervous as a kid on their first day of school. Several weeks into the season, the league's organizer asked me and a fellow teammate if we wanted to play in a skirmish between periods to promote women's hockey in Canada. We took one look at each other and then looked back at him, saying simultaneously, "Of course!" Our answer popped out before either of us could even think about what that meant.

Canada's National Women's Team was playing in a four-nation tournament against the United States, Finland, and Sweden. Their goal was to promote women's hockey in Canada. They were assembling two teams of women, over forty years of age, who were playing hockey for the first time. So, here we were, two rookie hockey players in our forties who were now going out to play hockey in front of thousands of spectators on national TV. Were we nuts? No, just gutsy, crazy, and playful, and we were going to have fun!

What an inspiring time that was for me. In that moment not only was I proud to step onto the ice in front of thousands of people, but I was also proud of myself for having taken the risk, stepping out beyond my comfortable boundaries, and just going for it. You are never too old to play hockey, and you are never too old to do anything else you want to do.

I have a long list of "to-do's" before I die, which I work on every day. I had no idea that trying to prove to my kids I could play hockey would give me so much more from the experience. Not only did I learn how to play hockey, but, more important, I also learned I could push myself and accomplish anything. This experience was rewarding on so many levels, and it continues to be a cherished time in my life. I checked "play hockey" off my bucket list!

Lesson #3: Be Nice to Everyone You Meet. One of my favourite bosses, whom I admired and respected tremendously, used to say, "Better be nice on your way up, because you never know who you will meet on your way down." To this day, I often use that line. To me, it's not just a great networking tip, it's a way of life. Throughout our lives and careers, we have both good and bad times. Regardless of what we are going through, it costs nothing to be nice to everyone. You never know who you are talking to or who they know. And even though they may be cold, or even rude, you never know what kind of day they're having. They may remember you as the only smile they received that day.

In the bank I managed a large staff, and it was part of my job to coach them on a regular basis. The people who knew me best were not the higher-ups, but the people I coached. These same people have been my best sources of referrals since going into business for myself. Why? Because they know me, we have a relationship, and they've experienced first-hand my coaching abilities. They provide awesome testimonials to my coaching skills and are a great source of referrals. Their confidence in me is a great reminder of the tremendous affect we have on the people in our lives, whether we know it or not.

Lesson #4: Be Giving. Over time, and certainly as a small business owner, I've learned networking is ongoing and a way of life. It's not about how many cold calls you made today, how many meetings you booked, or how many new clients you signed. Networking is about giving **and** receiving. Not about giving **in order** to receive.

In my initial stages of professional coaching, I met with a former banking colleague who entered the coaching profession a few years prior to me. She freely shared her thoughts and advice on entering this business. She was a terrific mentor to me, and while I have not had the opportunity to reciprocate her invaluable mentorship, I have freely given to others who have come after me. It's good karma.

Lesson #5: Build Your Relationship Database. Six degrees of separation? Truth or fiction? I'm not sure, but I'm amazed at how many people I know. I thought my contacts stayed with the corporate world, but, to my amazement and delight, this wasn't the case at all. I assembled my contacts (Rolodex, business card holders, address book, and email addresses) and sorted through them determining the "who, what, where, and when" of how I met them, as well as the last contact made.

After consolidation, I entered them all into Microsoft Outlook. With over two hundred names in my contacts database, I felt I had a good start, or so I thought. I barely knew some of the names and had a difficult time recalling faces to match the names, but today I am extremely proud of my connections (well over five hundred and counting), which are much stronger than the previously smaller number. What is the difference? I now understand the power of networking and the difference it makes, not only to my business but also to the quality of my life. I've not only expanded the source of referrals but also have a multitude of friendships that I have nurtured and developed. I encourage you to not underestimate the power of networking and its benefits in your life.

As a newbie entrepreneur, one of my strategies was to reconnect with some of the people from my past. In some cases, they were former colleagues who had moved on to other companies or other careers. Others were former suppliers or customers with whom I had formed a casual friendship. Most welcomed me with open arms, eager to reconnect, share their stories, and provide me with helpful hints, tips, advice, and referrals.

Today, I belong to a variety of networking groups. Often, I'm asked if joining networking clubs or groups is a valuable business-building strategy. I can answer definitively for myself. I choose to participate in networking groups where I enjoy the people in the group. It has to be enjoyable for me, and I have to like the people. Whether I receive business or not is secondary. I go for different reasons, and I meet a variety of interesting people, many of whom have interesting services that I can use or can refer to others. I have an array of colleagues who share the entrepreneurial spirit and have given me great ideas for building and managing my business. And, yes, occasionally I get some business too. Effective relationship-building networking takes time and energy.

Lesson #6: Communicate, Communicate, Communicate. One of my (many) learned lessons is the importance of regular and consistent communication. Sporadic communications with big-time gaps are of little value. When I began my business, one of my first acts was to craft an email and send it to everyone in my database, letting them know where I was and what I was doing. This email helped me to do the following things:

- Determine if my contact information for them was up to date
- Act as a subtle way to let the recipients know that I was open to any referrals they might think me worthy of
- Lay the foundation and create expectations for future updates, newsletters, or offers that I might send them

This was very worthwhile, and I reconnected with a number of people I thought I had lost track of. I also received much positive feedback and support about what I was embarking on. I even got some business!

I maintain regular contact with my network by sending out promotional offers for my services, periodic updates on new information I've learned, or information about any of my new activities. Communication can be a simple phone call, a referral, a quick email, a flyer, face-to-face contact, or workshop notices. It is important to communicate regularly and to stay connected. When was the last time you received a personal email from someone you met at an event, who wrote to say how nice it was to have met you? Even a simple email like, "Hey, I was wondering how you are doing?" goes a long way.

Lesson #7: Set Networking Goals. I'm a natural goal-setter. Even as a child, I set goals. If you have a clear vision in your head, the rest falls into place. I don't have a detailed business plan. At the beginning of each new year, I set three to four goals for the year and keep them close to my computer and visible. I review them daily. This helps me to stay focused and to do the actions that move me toward my goals. Anything else is just not as important.

Lesson #8: Keep it Simple. Regarding networking activities, I maintain the same "keep it simple" mindset. I look for opportunities to meet interesting people whom I can learn from, have fun with, or help, or who can connect me to others. When I meet them, I engage in interesting conversation, and if they are someone I would like to build a further relationship with, I ask them for a business card. On the back of the card, I record something to jog my memory, or maybe even something I've committed to follow up with them on. Often I can connect them to someone I know who might be helpful, refer a good book, or direct them to an interesting article or website. I like to connect on a personal level and find that others like that too. All of my new connections are quickly added to my database, and I also record where I met them as well as any other pertinent information about them.

Lesson #9: Build Rapport Magically. I like to attend events I enjoy, rather than events that may be good for business. Why? Because I'm attracted to like-minded individuals. It's about the people. I'm a "people-focused" person in a "people-focused" business. As a professional coach, people have to like or, at least, be comfortable with me. So the ability to build rapport quickly and easily is a very important skill, not only in the business of coaching but also in building any lasting relationship.

Are you a people magnet or a people repellent? What are you projecting outwardly? Do people see you as a positive, warm, and friendly person when they look at or interact with you, or does your negativity push them away? In a business or networking event, some wear their game face, pretending to be friendly and likeable. When they are at the hockey arena, however, watching their kid play, they may be yelling profanities. Or you may be somewhere outside their work environment and ask them how they are. Their reply may be something negative like, "Oh, I hate my job."

Is this the person you want to give business to or refer your best client or friend to? What I realized long ago is that who I am as a person is (and should be) the same, whether in the work setting or in the personal setting. I'm the same person, and my image, brand, essence, or whatever you want to call it is me all the time. While I can't control what happens to me, I can control my response or reactions, and that makes all the difference to me and the person others see me as. Adopt a consistent persona — be someone people can rely on to always be the same — and not only will your business grow, but your life will be better too.

Lesson #10: Access Available Resources. You wear multiple hats when you own your own business. During my first year, I was the receptionist, accounts payable and receivable clerk, customer service department, technology guru, marketing expert, and CEO. At times, it was overwhelming. I missed my corporate assistant and the ability to call the IT department when my computer froze in the middle of an email. Working for myself, however, has numerous advantages that vastly override all the things I miss. I enjoy setting my own deadlines and having the freedom of total creative licence over my marketing material, my website, my logo, and anything else that is my brand. And, over time, I've come to appreciate that everything I had in my corporate world is easily accessible through the power of my own network. So remember, you may feel alone, but, in fact, there are many resources available, and sometimes it's only a matter of asking the right questions or asking them of the right people.

For me, networking is a way of being, a part of who I am in my life. The world presents us with one opportunity after another. People come into and leave our lives as if on cue, and since I believe everything happens for a reason and that every person we meet is there to fulfill our purpose, I'm always curious about who I meet and cross paths with. Why are they there at that specific point in time and at that particular place? It is much more than just the machinations of a networking event; it may be karma, fate, serendipity, providence, the law of attraction at work, or whatever label you wish to ascribe.

Keeping this perspective helps me to play in a larger arena of my life. Networking for me is an integral and vital part of my life's journey. Everyone I meet and interact with matters in the larger scheme of my life, even though I may not know how or why at that moment. They are another piece of the puzzle that is my life; I just need to find the right place for them to fit. I believe I manifest everything in my life, including the failures that I learn from and the successes I celebrate. So when I coincidently bump into a former corporate client at the hockey arena, I am happy to see them, and I believe it is truly meant to be.

About Linda Cattelan

LINDA CATTELAN is a professional life coach, speaker, and writer.

With over twenty-five years' worth of corporate experience, including twelve years at the executive level, Linda Cattelan is a catalyst and change leader who enhances individual and team performance. Linda has a superior track record in coaching and mentoring both individuals and teams to consistently achieve outstanding business results.

Recognized as an expert in the field of coaching and mentoring, Linda is a featured guest on TV shows such as Life by Design, has been nominated for the Mentor of the Year Award, and has provided content and editorial support to Human Resources Development Canada for the development of "Mentoring for Business Organizations."

In addition to having a Master's of Business Administration, Linda is a certified trainer and master practitioner in neuro-linguistic programming (NLP) and a Certified Professional Co-Active Coach (CPCC).

Guiding Individuals and Teams to Excellence

Please visit Linda at
www.resultscatalyst.ca

Chapter XXII

SPENDING THE SIXPENCE: AN INTROVERT'S GUIDE TO NETWORKING

BY IRENE ANDERSON

Chapter XXII

SPENDING THE SIXPENCE: AN INTROVERT'S
GUIDE TO NETWORKING
by Irene Anderson

"Ninety percent of this game is half mental."
— Yogi Berra

"You should be more outgoing. Just speak up!" If I had a dollar for every time I heard those words, I would be rich beyond my wildest imagination. But I am an introvert by nature, and asking this of me is to ignore the very essence of who I am. Introversion is innate, an inborn preference, just like being left or right-handed — one is more dominant. Introversion is not about being socially awkward or shy. It is about how an individual's brain is wired and the mental processes that determine how he or she relates to the world.

The business world is filled with successful introverts who utilize networking to achieve their goals. The art of making connections to the people who can enhance our success is simply a matter of learning the strategies that work for our unique personality type.

My nature made me a bit of an enigma within my family. I was the "brain" of my Scottish family — the youngest — and a dreamer, living within a world of make-believe and happiest with my nose in a book or playing with my dolls. My mother, with five children to raise by herself after my dad died, couldn't really understand me. She was a structured, linear thinker; her step-by-step attempts to teach me how to tie my shoelaces and tell time were, well, nothing short of dramatic. I just didn't get it! Of course, I finally learned, but in my own non-linear, exploratory way. I can still see her shaking her head. I was just not like her, did not learn like her, and did not think like her.

All of our lives people will try to shape us introverts to "be like them." Resist this! Be yourself. When you do so, magic begins to happen in your life. There is absolutely nothing like the joy that is in your heart when you are being your authentic self.

SPENDING THE SIXPENCE: AN INTROVERT'S GUIDE TO NETWORKING

"It was a once-in-a-lifetime opportunity…and I've had a couple of those."
— Yogi Berra

MY VERY FIRST formal opportunity to network happened at the tender age of five when we were living in Scotland. One night, my mum pressed a sixpence into my palm and said, "Here you go, join the Brownies, they meet tonight at the church." I thought, Is she suggesting that I join by myself? Yes, she was, and she marched me out the door. So off I went, counting every step as if it were my last, even though the church was only a block away. You would have thought my destination was the guillotine.

I didn't want to go; fear of the unknown was haunting my every step. I didn't know how to get past that critical point: Walking through the door. I felt I just didn't want to be there, with all that noise and bustle. I would have been happier playing dolls with a couple of close friends. But my mum was a force to be reckoned with, and I didn't dare disobey her.

In those days, it was perfectly acceptable to send a young child out by herself, and so I arrived alone at the local church where the Brownies met. I stood outside, petrified to go in. My head was running a two-sided conversation: *Go on, go in — you'll have fun! No, I can't, I don't know anyone. Mum says you should go. But what if they don't like me?* This is what it can be like inside the head of an introvert.

I never did enter that church; I sat outside, looking through the window, watching the Brownies play games and have fun. When my mum came to fetch me, there I stood, clutching my sixpence. She just shook her head, took my hand, and, to my relief, off we went home.

Okay, I was only five at the time, but the memory stays with me as a reminder of what opportunities we can miss out on in life if we don't push ourselves outside our comfort zones. For introverts, taking that first step can be mind-numbing, but just imagine the great friends I could have made if only I had plucked up the courage to walk through those doors.

My extroverted daughter is quite the opposite. On her first day of school, I was the anxious one; she nearly pulled my arm off trying to hurry up and get inside. She couldn't wait. She made new friends within minutes of arriving at the school. Stunned, I assumed that, like me, she would be reticent (and, of course, miss her mommy all morning!). That night, I heard about every kid in her class — she is a natural talker and has not stopped since she learned how. I am constantly amazed at her outgoing nature and the number of people she has gathered around her.

Introverts are in the minority in North American society (about 25 percent). More often than not, introverts are overlooked or ignored. Many find they may say something profound or funny at a meeting or party but get no response — only to hear it repeated by someone else (usually an extrovert), with everyone assuming it was their original idea. If you are an introvert, like me, you've no doubt experienced this. If you are an extrovert, however, read on to learn how to help your introverted sisters thrive in an extroverted world.

According to Dictionary.com, an introvert is defined as:

- A shy person
- A person characterized by concern, primarily with his or her own thoughts and feelings

Extrovert is defined as:

- An outgoing, gregarious person
- A person characterized by extroversion; a person concerned primarily with the physical and social environment

Doesn't the extrovert definition look more appealing? That's because in our North American culture, being an introvert is not considered acceptable. The definitions were probably written by an extrovert! One truly interesting fact is that, when you search for the term "introvert" on Dictionary.com, three links to self-help websites appear — but none appear when you search for the term "extrovert." According to Dictionary.com, then, extroverts need no help, but introverts are in serious need of "fixing."

So which one are you? This is fairly simple to determine: Extroverts draw their energy from other people and outside stimulation; introverts draw their energy from inner stimulus. Extroverts feel drained of energy if they are not around people, while introverts feel drained if they are around people too much. Neither is right or wrong, fixed or broken, best or worst, good or bad. The labels only delineate our style of relating to the world outside ourselves.

So, how can introverts survive and thrive in an extroverted world? My advice to fellow introverts is to seek out and accept opportunities to speak in public. Share your personal experience, passion, and expertise, and this will open up many opportunities.

"I really didn't say everything I said."
— Yogi Berra

SPENDING THE SIXPENCE: AN INTROVERT'S GUIDE TO NETWORKING

MY FIRST SPEAKING engagement was before a group of public sector employees out on strike in the early '80s. They wanted someone to address their mostly female membership about being on strike — how it was not scary. Ha! What a tall order. Being on strike is both the scariest and the most liberating experience anyone could ever have.

As a telephone operator, I had just returned from a seventeen-week strike that made national history. How could I tell a group of women not to worry, that "It will all work out"? I knew the stress that they were experiencing, and that their families were urging them to get back to work. I had to somehow encourage them to keep going, to stand their ground.

To my surprise, this speaking gig was to take place outside in the freezing cold, with me standing on top of a car! Not exactly the "place to be" for an introvert. But I rose to the occasion, spit out my "barnburner," and jumped down from the car to resounding applause. I have no idea what I said that day. I was shaking like a leaf, and not just from the cold. Did I mention that I am afraid of heights, too? But I survived — and they loved me! I loved myself too, for pushing myself to do what I needed to do, for surviving the experience, and for growing as a result.

That event started the notion among my union sisters and brothers that I loved to speak in public, and they began volunteering me. My next adventure was at an International Women's Day Parade, in the middle of University Avenue, on top of one of those stone pots that contain trees and flowers, talking about women's rights. For the entire twenty years I spent as a union activist, I was asked repeatedly to speak about similar subjects. Thankfully, not all of them were from great heights!

"He's learning me his experience."
— Yogi Berra

TAKE ADVANTAGE OF any and all speaking engagements available to you. I was once told by a passionate humanitarian, "Never telegraph your shots." In other words, don't let people know that you are quaking in your boots. Sort of like "Never let them see you sweat." I've carried this advice with me always. Taking some public-speaking courses and joining Toastmasters helped me to refine my speaking skills.

Remember that everyone gets nervous (even extroverts) — so learn the tricks to control it. Breathing helps! So does practice, practice, practice! Know that you have a special purpose on this planet: Share it with everyone, pluck up your courage, and go for it. You will exceed your own expectations.

In my younger days, if you were to ask some people who knew me, they would tell you that I was an outspoken pain in the neck — but definitely not an introvert. I appeared on television, exposing health and safety issues in the call centre where I worked, spoke at conventions of more than two thousand delegates, and travelled to Mexico and throughout the United States to teach other trade unionists how to mobilize their memberships. I taught union courses, spoke at picket lines, and fought for just about every cause. In my extensive involvement in the labour movement, I had a reputation for being unafraid to take on the "establishment." But I was still an introvert by nature. That never changed.

So how did an acknowledged introvert pull this off? One word: **Passion.** I honestly believed in every cause I advocated for, and this convinced others to follow me. There is no other way to explain how I was able to get up on my feet and mobilize my audiences. Introverts, this is how you will find your voice: Find a product, service, or cause you really believe in, and your passion will shine through. Passion trumps fear every time. Everyone has felt stuck or afraid at some point — but take action, and it will soon dispel any fears you may be harbouring.

If you are very lucky, your ideal client may show up to hear you speak, or even walk right into your office. But you will also need to get out there and let other potential clients know about your product or services. For introverts, networking can be an intimidating minefield. Below are five valuable tips to help you navigate your way through.

"Pair up in threes."
— Yogi Berra

Pair up with a friend, ask her to introduce you with a tag line or joke, and do the same for her. I have a friend who does this naturally; she always introduces me like this: "Hi, so-and-so, this is Irene. She has done such and such." Make sure your introduction is interesting and funny, if possible. This opens the door for the other person to ask about you, and, once the conversation begins, you are on a roll. It's a great way to enter into a conversation as well as help the introvert move past that first hurdle. Now, the trick is to keep the conversation going. Be on your toes, listening for cues about other subjects you can transition to. Don't drop the ball.

Have something to talk about! It's a challenge for introverts to find something to talk about. We just don't feel the need for social chatter. You can always spot the introvert around the office water cooler. (Well, they probably won't be there in the first place!) But if they get caught at that unlikely spot, they quickly tire of the chatter about last night's episode of the latest reality show and are the first to slip away.

When you run out of steam, ask the other person a question about themselves. Learn something about the other person, and make it all about them. Get to know the person you are conversing with by asking about their business, family, favourite sports team, and so forth. Remember, people love to talk about themselves! Be a good listener, asking probing and open-ended questions (avoid questions that can be answered with a simple yes or no).

Be who you are. Everyone is unique; however, according to twenty-five centuries of personality-type theory, there are four primary types. There are many different models that explain this, but I have based the following descriptions on David Keirsey's model (visit www.personalityzone.com for more information). Listed below are some points about each type, and how to network effectively. The key is to find something that you are comfortable with. Focus on positive social networking, offering your help and services — and the opportunities will be presented to you.

- **GOLD — (needs membership and belonging; values family and tradition).** Golds do best with networking opportunities where they can bring value to business operations or volunteer groups. Offer your strong organizational skills — updating the filing system, or sorting out all that endless paperwork — and satisfy both your need and your networking goals.

- **ORANGE — (needs freedom to act, to seize opportunities without restriction).** Share your rebellious streak! Look for networking opportunities where your natural troubleshooting and negotiating skills will energize people to action. You like to have fun! Share a skill you have — for example, teach a course.

- **BLUE — (needs meaningful, empathetic relationships; strong cooperative skills).** Look for networking opportunities where you can help organizations or individuals succeed. Use all that time you've spent browsing the self-help section of your favourite bookstore — start up a peer-coaching group!

- **GREEN — (needs to learn constantly and to be seen as competent).** Look for networking opportunities where you can help others see the "big picture," sharing new ideas and strategies. Offer your exceptional research skills, and become an authority on the subject. Write a book! Help others with writing skills, but remember to lighten up a bit and have fun!

Act As If. Are you an innie or an outie? Often clients say to me, "I'm a bit of both." Okay, I can go along with that, but extroversion is seen to be the more favourable trait. So we often adopt the "Be more outgoing — you'll get ahead faster" approach. Easier said than done for an introvert: "Acting as if" you are an extrovert can be exhausting.

But the reality is this: You have to survive in an extroverted world. As an entrepreneur, you must get out and meet people if you want to create success for your business. So learn the game, but don't be untrue to yourself. When you do talk, make it about something for which you feel a real passion, and it will be naturally fascinating for your listeners. Remind yourself about all of the great skills you have and the things you know — and share them! It's okay to "act as if" when passion is driving you.

Take small steps. In a scene in the film Nobody's Fool, a young introverted boy is frightened when his grandfather forgets him and leaves him outside a house in the snow. That night, the grandfather gives the boy a stopwatch. He says, "Do you think you can be brave for one minute?" The boy looks uncertain, but finally says yes. The grandfather says, "Then start by being brave for just one minute, then next time two, and then the next time you won't be scared at all."

This is the key, fellow introverts: Embrace the uniqueness that is you! Just be brave for one minute at a time, and take little steps. Soon you will be walking into any networking event, head held high, no longer "acting as if" but being truly confident in the moment. It's not about learning to be less introverted, but about taking what works for you and then working the room. Reward your successes as well; think of small ways that you can congratulate yourself for getting out of your comfort zone.

Learning to network effectively is a gift you give to yourself; it's about reaching beyond what you already know. It brings a sense of accomplishment and a tremendous increase in your self-confidence. You'll be energized and thrilled by how much people are willing to help you on your journey.

When you share your unique gifts, abundance will come to you. If you don't show up, the world has missed your gifts. How all those little Brownies did in life, I'll never know, for it was an opportunity I missed. So every day, I try to stretch myself out of my comfort zone — even if I am being brave for only a minute. I know my purpose; I am compelled to share and help.

So, my introverted friends, *pluck* up your courage, unfurl your fingers, and open your hand: ***Go out and spend the sixpence!***

About
Irene
Anderson

IRENE ANDERSON is the director of DiscoveryWorks! Training and Coaching. Irene's passion is helping people maximize their true potential. She is an experienced facilitator and consultant in the areas of interpersonal communication, team building, career development, and personal success.

Irene leverages her expertise with a variety of assessments to help her clients improve their ability to interact with others more effectively. Some of the assessments she uses include the Myers-Briggs Type Indicator® (MBTI®), Personality Dimensions®, True Colors®, and Interstrength®.

"The self-help gurus tell you to find your life purpose, follow your passion, and live your values. However, with all of the socialization and 'fitting in' we do all of our lives, we tend to lose sight of who we really are inside."

Irene can help you unlock that secret key to living your life purpose and understanding yourself and others. She is passionate about encouraging people to achieve their maximum potential while having fun. Her facilitation style is high energy and fun.

Please visit
www.discoveryworkscoaching.com

MOVING FORWARD...
- CONTINUOUS GROWTH FOR FUTURE SUCCESS

This powerful book is bound by a common theme — a connective tissue that is woven into each contributing author's words. You have experienced a sharing of intimacies and a glimpse into each author's private experiences and journeys. The ladies in *The Power of Women United* impart the many ways their individualism leads to similarities. Their words of wisdom will not only resonate with you but, more important, also give you an insight into opening up your own world. In many ways, after reading this book, you'll feel a deep sense of connection with each one of these phenomenal women.

These incredible women share their stories, openly and honestly, in the hopes of making your journey easier than theirs have been. By reading and understanding the lessons they share in these pages, our hope is that something has resonated with you to give you the strength and encouragement to live your dreams and achieve your desires.

The Power of Women United is about possibilities and offers a light, a beacon, to help illuminate your way. Grasp the concept that everyone has the equal opportunity to achieve success in whatever way they want, however it is defined for that individual. In each of our lives, there are moments that we can say shaped who we are now, and if we stop long enough to realize the lessons, we have been truly blessed by them.

You will find you are not alone as you discover that many a great "ordinary woman" has walked the same path as you and has lived the struggles you may have lived or are living through now. Each of these women have shared pivotal moments and experiences, turning them into lessons that have shaped who they are now, so that you may benefit from their understanding and knowledge. Stories of others' lives give us strength and inspiration to move forward, and give us pause to explore our own journey and story. This book is an invaluable reference guide you can turn to again and again as a source of motivation and encouragement at times when you are facing challenges as you continue your journey to create your good-better-best life.

As you have read, the ladies in this book have all come from diverse backgrounds and experiences, but their lessons have many parallel threads. We are certain that segments of this book have spoken to you in distinct ways that may differ from the experiences of others reading it; however, one of the main themes is about developing confidence. Building inner confidence in knowing you are doing the best you can is fundamental to your success in life. Gaining confidence that you can communicate and network in effective ways that make sense for you is a key message imparted on these pages.

Some of the chapters offer you practical information and tools you can start using immediately, while others are slanted a bit more toward personal self-discovery. In either case, you'll be able to relate all of the chapters to your own life; you may even adopt some bits of introspection and fully integrate them into your world. Listening to and following your heart is critical to knowing where you want to go with your life. Paying attention to the whispers we hear along the way keeps us on track and helps us avoid getting the figurative hit on the head with the brick to get the message we need to hear.

Continually learning and improving upon what we know, are, and do keeps us current and also helps us feel energized and empowered. A positive self-image is born of a conscious willingness to create and recreate whom we want the world to see. Again, confidence is vital to this. We must also not lose the true essence of who we are at our core. Acting with caution toward conformity, our willingness to fit in to what others say is the ideal, will usually compromise who we really are and who we want to be, and provide more struggles than we should be experiencing. Be cognizant of others' opinions and how you allow them to permeate your ideas of who you really are. Stay true to yourself while showing the world what wonderful things you have to offer.

Change is inevitable in life, and the more we accept it as a positive element, the more peaceful we will be with all its complicated parts. Change can lead to wonderful things if we are open to it. It is necessary for growth and self-development. There is a speed in which life moves forward, challenging us to reposition our thinking, pushing us to have the courage to see what needs to change within us and in our outer world in order to keep advancing with it.

The Power of Women United is a testament to the true POWER in women uniting and compiling their thoughts and ideas to pass on to others so they may gain insight and accelerate their paths to clarity for themselves and their dreams. Our collective hope is that you have received as much pleasure and enlightenment from reading this book as we have received in creating it for you.

COMING SOON!

The Power of Young Women is a brilliant tribute to all women who embrace the opportunity to communicate what they have learned in relating to each other. Focusing on mature women together with their younger counterparts, the authors will impart to you the beauty in the female-to-female relationship. Sharing their experiences as seen through both sets of eyes, we learn what it means to open our minds to mentoring and learning from each other.

Your Opportunity to Continue Your Journey!

The Power of Women Exchange is proud to be a portal for women who are seeking to expand their horizons, to share their successes, and to grow personally and professionally. If you would like to grow or to offer women in your area an opportunity, consider opening a POWE chapter near you. Please visit www.powe.ca for more information.

May all the blessings this life has to offer be yours!

Tina Dezsi and Lia Bandola

The Ultimate
Publishing
House

www.tuphpublishing.com

email:
admin@tuphpublishing.com

contact:
647 883 1758